'This is a brilliantly insightful and much needed study by one of Wales' leading historians, using a range of sources including her own personal memories of Port Talbot and its stars'

Hywel Francis, historian

'This is an important work that deepens our sense of a changing Wales... nicely combining local with international and popular with scholarship'

Peter Stead, author of Acting Wales

'Tremendous... it tells a fascinating and very important story and does so in a way that will be accessible to a very wide readership'

Chris Williams, editor of The Richard Burton Diaries

'Local knowledge is the foundation of this well-researched and very readable account. Richard Burton and Company are the stars but Angela John shows just how they came to attain that celestial state'

Sally Roberts Jones, Port Talbot historian

'In this stimulating book... Angela John does well to link "these fiery, mercurial and unpredicatable" actors with the physical landscape that produced them'

Daily Mail Book of the Week

T0169082

Angela V. John is a widely published historian and biographer living in Pembrokeshire but originally from Port Talbot. She held the chair in History at the University of Greenwich for many years and is currently an honorary professor at Swansea University. Previous publications include the award-winning *Coalmining Women* (Cambridge University Press) and a biography of the Ibsenite actress, suffragette and novelist: *Elizabeth Robins: Staging A Life 1862-1952* (Routledge and The History Press). Her most recent book is *Turning the Tide: The Life of Lady Rhondda* (Parthian). She is a vice-president and former chair of Llafur: The Welsh People's History Society.

www.angelavjohn.com

THE ACTORS' CRUCIBLE

THE
ACTORS'
CRUCIBLE

Port Talbot and the Making of Burton,
Hopkins, Sheen and All the Others

ANGELA V. JOHN

PARTHIAN

Parthian, Cardigan SA43 1ED
www.parthianbooks.com
First published in 2015
© Angela V. John 2015
ISBN 978-1-910409-94-7
Edited by Francesca Rhydderch
Typeset by Elaine Sharples
Printed at Dinefwr Press, Llandybie
Published with the financial support of the Welsh Books Council
British Library Cataloguing in Publication Data
A cataloguing record for this book is available from the British Library.

For Andrew, Mair, Nia, Andrew H. and Katie

with gratitude and love

CONTENTS

ACKNOWLEDGEMENTS

This subject crept up on me and took me over. I had embarked on another project, a more conventional historical study. But a chance meeting with Michael Sheen at a conference got me thinking. Back in 2010 in a survey article called 'Lifers: Modern Welsh History and the Writing of Biography' (in the *Welsh History Review*) I had floated the idea of someone writing about the remarkable cluster of actors from Port Talbot and a few years later, to my surprise, hijacked myself and embarked on what became *The Actors' Crucible*.

So my first thank you must be to my publisher Richard Davies at Parthian for generously permitting me to deviate (temporarily) from the volume he had been expecting in order to research and write this book. I am grateful also to Gillian Griffiths, Claire Houguez, Robert Harries, Elaine Sharples and Susie Wild. Thanks are due to William Howells. I am especially pleased to have had the opportunity to work again with the writer Francesca Rhydderch as my editor.

Many people have generously assisted me during the course of my research and I appreciate this. It would be impossible to list everybody here but I must mention the invaluable contribution of those who willingly subjected themselves to my interviews, usually in long sessions in their homes and/or in repeated written and oral communication. They are: Matthew Aubrey, Robert Blythe, Philip Bond, Di Botcher, Betty Brooks Richards, Rob Brydon, Katrina Burton, Norman Comer, Hubert Davies, Rona Davies, Godfrey Evans, Nick Evans, Helen John, Simeon Jones, Luke Joyce, Gary Lagden, Caroline Michael, Kevin Matherick, Francine Morgan, Siân Owen, Doug Rees, Kyle Rees, Matthew Rees, Carol Scott, Meyrick Sheen, Michael Sheen, Gareth Snook, Jean Thomas, Gwyn Thomas, Ken Tucker,

Michael Waters and Patricia Wright. Some of you also kindly supplied photographs.

Special thanks must go to Michael Sheen for his sustained encouragement. His parents Irene Sheen and Meyrick Sheen and uncle John Sheen have provided assistance in a host of ways. Thank you to Sir Anthony Hopkins for letting me use the signed photograph and to Roy Guy for allowing me to reproduce his portrait of the actor. I am also indebted to Nia John for her photography and Llewela Gibbons for her expertise. Thanks to John Adams, Alana Adye, Allen Blethyn, Allan Cook, Alan Davies, Rhian Davies, Amanda Duke, John V. Hughes, Ronald Jenkins, Doreen John, Elin Jones, Richard Jones, Sara Mays, Jeff Maddox, Pam Rees, Dennis Reed, Gaynor Richards, Shaun Richards, David Scott, Avril Stevens, Natalie Thomas, Lloyd Trott, Rhianon Trowell, Stephanie Ward and Heath Woodward for the information/sources/photographs they have supplied. Peter Whitebrook has been very helpful. Enfys McMurry kindly talked to Rosalie Mahoney in the United States and I am grateful to both of them. Every effort has been made to trace copyholders.

One of my greatest debts is to Fred and Marilyn Steadman-Jones who entrusted me with the precious archive they have built up for Cyril Jenkins. Fred has also answered numerous queries with patience and good humour. And I am especially grateful to Sally Burton for letting me use the Burton-Burgess correspondence in the National Library of Wales and for permitting me to reproduce a page of Richard Burton's early diary. Thanks as well to Swansea University for allowing me to consult the original diaries and correspondence in the Richard Burton Papers held in the university's Richard Burton Archive. I thank Elisabeth Bennett, university archivist and her staff and Steve Williams. Paula Durnell and staff at Dyffryn School, where the archives

Acknowledgements

for the Sec are kept, were welcoming and helpful, as were staff and pupils at Sandfields School. Thanks also to Gill Lewis, Mayor's Secretary, Mayor's Parlour, Port Talbot. I appreciate the assistance of Andy Brown at Port Talbot YMCA and thank the librarians and archivists at the following: Bristol University (Theatre Collection), the British Library, the BBC Written Archives Centre, Caversham Park, Reading (Matthew Chipping), the BFI Library, Cardiff Central Library, Haverfordwest Library, Port Talbot Library, Taibach Library and West Glamorgan Archives. As always, the staff at the National Library of Wales have been unfailingly helpful. I am grateful as well to those at RWCMD Cardiff, RADA, and Central who answered queries and to Catrin Rogers at NTW.

Sally Roberts Jones and Professors Hywel Francis, Peter Stead and Chris Williams kindly read my manuscript and I greatly value their informed comments. Finally, I would like to thank the historian Professor Ieuan Gwynedd Jones. I have known him since I was a raw postgraduate student of his at Swansea University. He is now in his nineties but when he was young he lived and worked in Port Talbot. We have had valuable conversations about the town's history and its people. I cherish this abiding friendship and Ieuan's knowledge and wisdom.

ILLUSTRATIONS

Cover: Richard Burton (Siân Owen); Anthony Hopkins (by Edward Russell Westwood/© estate of Russell Westwood, National Portrait Gallery, London); Michael Sheen (Sarah Dunn/www.sarahdunn.com)

15. Anthony Hopkins (Tony) expresses his gratitude to Cyril Jenkins (Anthony Hopkins, Cyril Jenkins Archive)

16. The young Godfrey Evans as Becket in Selwyn Davies' school production (Dyffryn School Archives)

17. 'Once in a Lifetime', WGYTC production, 1985. Maxine Evans, Darren Lawrence (Port Talbot), Karen Willans, Michael Sheen (Port Talbot), Buddug Morgan (Kevin Matherick)

18. Dennis Burgess (Peter Stevens)

19. Ivor Emmanuel (the Emmanuel family)

20. Robert Blythe (Robert Blythe)

21. Di Botcher (Di Botcher)

22. Rob Brydon (Trevor Leighton)

23. Siân Owen and her uncle Richard Burton (Angela V. John)

24. The Portrait Bench on the Richard Burton Trail: Richard Burton, Rob Brydon and Forest Ranger Dick Wagstaff (Siân Owen)

25. Norman Comer (Norman Comer)

26. Godfrey Evans, founder of WGYTC at its 40th anniversary celbrations in Port Talbot, 2015 (Godfrey Evans/ WGYTC)

27. Glan Afan School Centenary production of *Under Milk Wood*, 1996. Professional actors and ex-pupils Michael Sheen and Norman Comer played 1st and 2nd Voice and local actor/producer Alan Davies was Captain Cat. Ken Tucker was the producer (Ken Tucker)

28. Sandfields School production of *Sweeney Todd* in 2003 with Marc Antolin and Christina Modestou (Helen John)

29. Sandfields School pupils rehearsing with their drama teacher Helen John for *The Wizard of Oz* 2015 (Sara Mays)

30. Michael Sheen (Sarah Dunn, www.sarahdunn.com)

31. Programme for *Behold The Man* (Carol Scott)

32. Carol Mends (assistant director), Ina D. Jones (producer and director) and Carol Scott (assistant director) attending a planning meeting for *Behold The Man* in Margam Park with Margam Castle in the background (David Scott)

33. *The Passion*: At the Seaside Social Club on the Saturday Night: Kyle Rees, Matthew Woodyatt, Francine Morgan, Michael Sheen, David Rees Talbot, Matthew Aubrey, John-Paul Macleod, Darren Lawrence. All these actors are from Port Talbot with the exception of Gwent's Matthew Woodyatt (Richard Hardcastle/National Theatre Wales)

34. *The Passion*: Michael Sheen as The Teacher in the crowd (Geraint Lewis/National Theatre Wales)

35. *The Passion*: Members of the Company on the Beach (Richard Hardcastle/National Theatre Wales)

ABBREVIATIONS

Arts Ed – Arts Educational, London

Central – Royal [since 2012] School of Speech and Drama, London

LAMDA – London Academy of Music and Dramatic Art

National – Royal [since 1988] National Theatre, South Bank, London

NTW – National Theatre Wales

RADA – Royal Academy of Dramatic Art

RSC – Royal Shakespeare Company

RWCMD – Royal [since 2002] Welsh College of Music and Drama, Cardiff

WGYTC – West Glamorgan Youth Theatre Company, Swansea

MAP

The Port Talbot District.

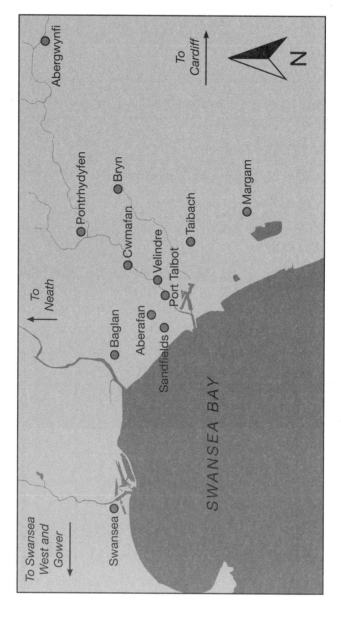

INTRODUCTION
Going to town

It is the place where the mountains almost meet the sea. It's the gritty industrial town that you can't ignore, positioned between the cities of Cardiff and Swansea on the south Wales coast. And it is renowned for producing famous actors. As the broadcaster Patrick Hannan put it, here is 'a golden triangle for the acting trade'.[1]

This book explores how and why this much-maligned steel town has generated a glittering array of men and women with careers in drama. It considers their early lives and their relationship to their community.

A triumvirate of Richard Burton, Sir Anthony Hopkins and Michael Sheen heads the cast. In 2005 a poll by the Old Vic Theatre named Hopkins the greatest British actor of all time (Lord Olivier came second) and Burton sixth.[1] For one Welsh town to have produced such revered performers is remarkable. Yet, as this book demonstrates, Port Talbot has spawned at least fifty professional or semi-professional actors since the inter-war years. They include esteemed Shakespearean performers, West End actors starring in plays such as *War Horse* and in popular musicals, familiar voices on radio and in Welsh, British and American television dramas and soaps, film actors across the decades and actors seasoned in repertory theatre. Then there is the actress who inspired Bette Davis and the actor who was the model for the character of Cliff Lewis in John Osborne's *Look Back in Anger*. A number of devotees of drama became teachers of the subject as well as moving into theatre production and

other related work. And there is a deep-rooted commitment to amateur theatre in the town.

On 4 June 2014 the *South Wales Evening Post* asked and answered its own question: 'Most talented place on earth? It must be Neath–Port Talbot'. This was, admittedly, an account of performers who had reached the finals in the television series *Britain's Got Talent* – most recently the thirteen-year-old local rapper Leondre Devries – but it also identified a wider Hall of Fame from the locality, naming fifteen individuals. Included was the Hollywood film star Ray Milland (1907–86) from Neath, the first Welsh actor to win an Academy Award. In 1945 he was Best Leading Actor for playing an alcoholic writer in *The Lost Weekend*.

Port Talbot has never been short of famous residents.[2] In his series editor's introduction to *Real Port Talbot* Peter Finch wrote: 'There's more fame here per street than in Cardiff and Swansea combined'.[3] But it is the remarkable cluster of actors that this book highlights. The *Post's* article reflects the pride that the place has in its performers. Even allowing for some latitude, two-thirds of the somewhat eclectic list is comprised of men and women renowned not only in Britain but also internationally.[4] This invites closer investigation.[5]

A place dominated by labour (or, at times, lack of it) and Labour, Port Talbot is, in some respects, a Valleys town that slips down to the seaside. Topographically striking, it is bounded by both mountains and coast. Yet it has traditionally been assigned the role of the 'baddie' in the biographies of its stars. Usually written by those from far away,[6] it has been presented as a place that, against the odds, produced creative spirits who hastened to escape from it.

An archetypal town of heavy industry with an unforgettable industrial skyline, it has inherited the insults heaped on Merthyr Tydfil in the nineteenth century and been portrayed as a version of Dante's Hell, a blot on the landscape. Such a view

has been encouraged by the presence of a motorway that looks down on the town and whisks drivers away from it. This motorway on stilts permits a dramatic glimpse of the steelworks that stretch for three and a half miles.

In 2014 the partial closure of one of the M4's main exits enhanced a sense that it was a place to pass through rather than stop off. The Works (as the steel plant is known) has been claimed – incorrectly it seems – as the inspiration for Ridley Scott's film *Blade Runner*.[7] What is certain is that it has helped to produce many of the industrial products that we rely upon, including those cars that flee the scene. In 1960 the town boasted Europe's largest integrated steelworks. Exuding its own dangerous beauty, it has played a visceral role in shaping how the town's actors have related to their native environment.

If you travel from north to south you can glimpse the area's variety and history. Set off from the stunningly beautiful Afan Valley, once the site of coalmining and the Oakwood Ironworks but now a Forest Park renowned for mountain bike trails. Travel from Pontrhydyfen – boasting both aqueduct and viaduct – south through the former copper hub of Cwmafan (the English Copper Company held sway from the early 1840s) and you come down to the heart of Port Talbot, named after the family who developed the docks[8] in the nineteenth century. The town grew from a creek port that exported coal and imported copper ore from Cornwall. Its old centre was Aberafan/Aberavon, once an 'Ancient' borough. It boasted a covered market and much else and is still the name of the Parliamentary constituency.[9] Now Aberafan is synonymous with the beach and its miles of golden sands. To its west is residential Baglan, site of the old Baglan Hall and a Norman church named after St Baglan. BP Chemicals was nearby but the area is now being reinvented as an Energy Park.

On the other side of town is Taibach, once known for its copper (smelted there from 1770). Taibach means Little

Houses, and here and across the town Port Talbot remains remarkably free of high-rise homes. Most inhabitants are used to houses rather than flats, as witnessed at the Sandfields Estate built in the mid-twentieth century to house workers at the Steel Company of Wales. Nothing, it seems, can challenge the skyline of the Works.

Beyond Taibach lies Margam, best known for the modern steelworks (though Port Talbot's steel production dates back to the start of the twentieth century). Margam also has a British Oxygen plant, but cheek by jowl with such industry are less prominent but much older features such as a twelfth-century Cistercian Abbey Church (the steelworks used to be called the Abbey Works). It was the medieval monks of Margam Abbey who started extracting iron and lead ore in the area. There is too the Celtic Wheel Cross of Conbelin and Margam Park with its deer, the ruins of a beautiful Chapter House, an elegant eighteenth-century Orangery and the neo-Gothic Margam Castle, once home to Britain's richest heiress, the Victorian Emily Talbot.

Port Talbot has been and remains a town of contradictions and distinct parts. The boy the world would come to know as Richard Burton was born in the Afan Valley's Welsh-speaking industrial village of Pontrhydyfen but spent his childhood and teenage years a few miles south in Taibach. Anthony Hopkins hailed from Margam but moved to Taibach. Michael Sheen grew up further west in Baglan. And an exploration of what Peter Stead has called 'the Port Talbot conveyor belt'[10] of acting talent needs to recognise that despite their identification with the town, its most renowned trio emanated from somewhat different districts and backgrounds. Their respective dates of birth – 1925, 1937 and 1969 – also helped to ensure that although they shared much, they faced in their youth rather different challenges and opportunities.

Their fortunes and those of other local actors have, nevertheless, been characterised by impressive cultural and

educational institutions. Yet Port Talbot has never been a place dominated by the elite. Its population is and has been overwhelmingly working class. In 1949, for example, a survey[11] of the occupations of 240 fathers of pupils in one of the town's two grammar schools revealed that only 15 per cent were white collar workers and this was just before the number of industrial workers (which had declined significantly in the 1920s) increased once more with the development of Sandfields, which became the second largest housing estate in Wales.

Those artistic figures who 'made it' might be best understood if seen as part of a rich culture and community that has, over time, encouraged creativity and aspirations, whilst their very success has in turn prompted a pride and desire to emulate. Rather than turning their backs on the place, the key players have been a spur and encouragement to younger generations from the same town. Michael Sheen has commented how it has a 'rich cinematic element. You live in Port Talbot with the living presence of Richard Burton... people are fiercely proud of that heritage.' He stresses that Burton and Hopkins 'made my dreams of becoming an actor just a little more possible.'[12]

The book is divided into two parts. Part One upsets traditional narratives. In place of the familiar hasty genuflection to childhood and youth followed by a spotlight on superstar lives, loves and careers, it looks at the 'Big Three' before they became famous, seeking to understand them in the context of their time, place and contemporaries. Publication coincides with the 90[th] anniversary of Richard Burton's birth on 10 November 1925 and this book appears thirty-one years after his premature death in 1984. So the first chapter looks at the 1930s and 1940s and asks how the Port Talbot schoolboy Richard Jenkins emerged as the actor Richard Burton.

The Richard Burton story is, of course, especially beloved of journalists and Port Talbot pundits and it shapes and reshapes itself as circumstances demand. At its worst it suggests a crude

rags-to-riches story.[13] But even when it is knowingly and carefully weighed up by historians and cultural critics, the early years inevitably feature as a means to an end, since it is the life in the limelight that demands interrogation. Peter Stead's analysis is partly concerned with what else Burton might have achieved and, unlike some, he is not simply concerned about the screen overtaking the stage.[14] Chris Williams' fine editing of the Richard Burton diaries reveals the actor's introspection interwoven with the public face but the fact that just one year of diaries exists for the Port Talbot period accentuates the emphasis on Burton rather than Jenkins.[15]

I'll be showing how Richard Jenkins and then, in the second chapter Anthony Hopkins, discovered the stage and I'll be seeking, in so far as is possible, to read the story forwards rather than backwards, putting these actors into the context of their home environments before their careers developed. More recently, the subject of Chapter Three, Michael Sheen, has been portrayed as inheriting their mantle. The theatre and film director Sam Mendes has commented that Sheen is 'Welsh in the tradition of Anthony Hopkins and Richard Burton: fiery, mercurial, unpredictable'.[16] Sheen's rise to fame is examined.

The three chapters in Part Two look at the relationship between these world-famous figures and Port Talbot. It also considers its wide range of actors. In many other towns just one of these individuals would be cited with pride as *the* local success story. Chapter Four begins by considering legacy: the impact of the mega-stars and the significance of emulation for the career of the quick-witted Rob Brydon, who grew up in Baglan.

Peter Stead has noted how:

> As a nation we publicly mourned the passing of our coal miners and our steel workers and yet we failed to appreciate the silent revolution that made us a nation of actors.[17]

The chapter's main focus, however, is on the town as a crucible for actors, following in the footsteps of earlier successes and creating what the journalist Doug Rees calls an 'unusual production line of people'. An Appendix lists fifty Port Talbot actors whose voices and faces have been heard and seen on radio, the professional stage and the big and small screen. Di Botcher, whose work ranges from Shakespeare to soap operas, comments how 'We take it for granted' that local people are actors. She adds that when she goes to town: 'I quite often bump into parents of professional actors in Poundland talking about the West End or somebody going over to Broadway'.

Chapters Five and Six explore how the international actors have handled and expressed their relationship to Port Talbot over the years, looking at how, in different ways, Richard Burton and Anthony Hopkins have remembered their old homes and given something back to their communities. Michael Sheen has commented that his job is all about observation and that 'Every character I do has something of Port Talbot in it'.[18] *The Passion*, the ultimate in site-specific theatre, was performed across Port Talbot over the Easter weekend in 2011. The town was described in the national press as 'one of the happiest places on Earth'[19] and *The Passion* judged 'one of the outstanding theatrical events not only of this year, but of the decade'.[20] Most of its professional cast came from Port Talbot.

The conclusion sums up the ingredients that went into making this town the actors' capital of Wales and considers its position at a time when opportunities for Welsh actors seem to be expanding yet funding cuts threaten initial training.

Most biographies of superstars have been written by journalists, film and theatre critics or by those who investigate the life stories of the rich and famous. This book draws on rich biographical material about the town's many and varied actors, much of it based on extensive interviews. It is also a biography

of a place from the inter-war years onwards by a biographer and historian from the town.

My brother and family still live there. My paternal grandmother, Margaret David, was born and grew up in what is known as 'The Sker',[21] a Taibach pub that the young Richard Burton used to frequent. Margaret David married a builder descended from the nonconformist minister and writer of Welsh hymns, Thomas Williams (1761–1844) of Bethesda'r Fro. My maternal grandmother's father Henry Walsh was of Welsh-Irish descent and had an ironmonger's shop in Cwmafan Road. He was a founder of the local Liberal Club, a member of the Progressive Party and twice mayor of the borough.

In my teens I knew well several generations of the large Jenkins family who lived in and around Port Talbot. Through them I met their most famous relative: Richard Burton. In my early twenties I moved to London where I taught in a sixth-form college. In what now seems like another life – and a curiously bifurcated one – I would spend time with Richard and Elizabeth whenever they were in London, at their suite in the Dorchester Hotel and later at Squire's Mount, Hampstead, and attend rushes and premieres of their films.

In my early childhood I had lived in Beechwood Road just a couple of streets from Anthony Hopkins' Margam home and my parents were friends of his parents. My aunt and uncle lived in Baglan, home to Michael Sheen.

What follows draws on a mix of theatre and local history, oral history and biographical history, with a sprinkling of personal reminiscence. Put together it provides an alternative way of looking at the cultural history of a town and a profession.

PART ONE

BEFORE THEY WERE FAMOUS

1

Becoming Burton

The birth of Richard Walter Jenkins in Pontrhydyfen on 10 November 1925 has been seen as the start of the town's association with the acting profession and fame. Yet this is not quite true. Some years earlier Peg Entwistle and Thomas Owen Jones had made an impact on the wider world. They are hardly household names today but their stories of burgeoning fame followed by early tragedy are truly dramatic.

Millicent Lilian Entwistle, known as Peg, was born in 1908 at 5 Broad Street in the centre of Port Talbot.[22] This was where her grandparents, the Stevensons, lived – John Stevenson was a metallurgist – and where her mother Emily grew up. Peg's uncle, who also lived in Broad Street, was the foundation organist and choirmaster at the imposing St Theodore's Church built by Emily Talbot in 1897 and named after her brother Theodore (who had earlier brought Peg's great-uncle Frank Richard Seaton to Margam Abbey as its organist and choirmaster). Peg's mother had come home for the birth. She returned to west London soon afterwards with the baby but the marriage to Robert Entwistle did not last.

Robert obtained custody of Peg, though she apparently visited Port Talbot quite often as a little girl. However, they moved to New York when she was six. Robert remarried, but the child's stepmother died from spinal meningitis and when she was fourteen her father was killed in a hit-and-run accident. Robert had been an actor and so too was his brother Charles, a

11

successful London and New York stage manager. Charles and his wife now took care of Peg and her half-brothers. She studied acting in Boston and, aged sixteen, got a walk-on part in a Broadway production of *Hamlet*. The seventeen-year-old Bette Davis saw her in Ibsen's *The Wild Duck* and later claimed that it was Peg Entwistle's performance that inspired her to become an actor. Aged eighteen, Entwistle met an actor called Robert Keith. She married him four days later. A messy divorce followed.

By 1932 she was in Los Angeles in a supporting role with the young Humphrey Bogart in *The Mad Hopes* at the Bellasco Theatre. She also secured a part in a film: David O. Selznick's thriller *Thirteen Women* starring Myrna Loy. But her scenes ended up on the cutting-room floor. Within months of arriving in Hollywood the twenty-four-year-old blue-eyed, platinum blonde actor had taken her own life and secured more fame, albeit posthumously, than she had enjoyed during her short life.

In September 1932, with the aid of a ladder, Peg Entwistle threw herself off the top of the H of the Hollywood Sign (then called Hollywoodland). It was two days before her body was found in a ravine. A suicide note stressed that a lot of pain could have been spared had she taken action sooner, implying that the many personal tragedies of her life had taken their toll rather than simply the loss of her part in the film. Just a few days after her death a letter arrived offering her a job at the Beverley Hills Playhouse. It was the part of a woman driven to suicide.

Recently Peg Entwistle's death has attracted renewed attention. In 2014 an outdoor screening of *Thirteen Women* was shown in Hollywood with proceeds going to the American Foundation for Suicide Prevention. A book, essays and a documentary have appeared about her and there is a projected movie. Here in the UK, Heath Woodward's musical *Goodnight September*[23] argues that, far from being a failure, she achieved

much as an actor. But even if we focus on Peg Entwistle's life rather than death, it is a long way from Broad Street to Broadway and beyond.

Close to Broad Street is Talcennau Road where, in 1912, Port Talbot Higher Elementary School for boys and girls had opened. Nine years later it had been upgraded to a secondary school and began preparing pupils for the Welsh Central Board's School Certificate and Higher School Certificate. One of the boys who passed his scholarship to the Sec (as it was known) in the 1920s was a collier's son from the Afan Valley village of Bryn.

Born in 1914, Thomas Owen Jones was coached in drama by the schoolmaster P. H. Burton. He recognised the acting potential of this tall, handsome youth who seems to have been especially keen on physics. Indeed, according to a younger cousin of Owen Jones, Philip Burton arrived in Bryn one day and offered to adopt the schoolboy actor. His parents apparently sent him away 'with a flea in his ear'. As is well known, History would, in a sense, soon repeat itself.

In his final year at school Burton cast him as Petrucio in the school production of *The Taming of the Shrew*. He gave a 'brilliant and memorable performance.'[24] The actors were rewarded with a spread in the school kitchen and a 2d bar of chocolate. Jones also played rugby for the school and during rehearsals, instead of protesting to Petrucio with the words 'You are marvellous forward', the boy playing Gremio declared: 'You are a marvellous forward'.[25]

Jones won a Leverhulme Scholarship to RADA in 1933 then toured Wales, England and Ireland in repertory as well as acting on the London stage, most notably at the Old Vic. During its famed 1936–7 season he worked with some of the best-known actors of the past, present and future. In the Festival for Shakespeare's Birthday he appeared with the Vanbrugh sisters Violet and Irene as well as with Laurence Olivier, Alec Guinness and Margaretta Scott. He was in *Love's Labour's Lost* with

Michael Redgrave and Rachel Kempson, *Twelfth Night* with Olivia and Jessica Tandy and *Henry V* with Guinness and Olivier.

Philip Burton recalls that Owen Jones was Laertes to Olivier's Hamlet and that he took the young actor's parents to London to see him in this part.[26] Yet it was Michael Redgrave who was cast as Laertes in Tyrone Guthrie's uncut production of *Hamlet* that season.[27] It was during this run that Olivier, uncannily anticipating the future, announced one night to the audience that 'A great actress has been born. Laertes has a daughter'.[28] Redgrave had just become the father of a baby called Vanessa. Owen Jones did at least deliver the first line of the play but with the minor part of the sentry Bernardo, a role he reprised when Guthrie took the play to Elsinore's Kronborg Castle.[29]

Owen Jones was an understudy for the part of Laertes (a fact that Burton omitted to mention)[30] but the talented young Welshman does seem to have had the chance to play Laertes at least once, and he was anyway appearing in Shakespeare's plays with the best. He might in time have become a household name. But after taking a commission as a wartime RAF flying officer, he damaged his hip when a packed parachute fell on him from a great height. Complications resulted in cancer and his death in December 1942, aged just twenty-eight.[31]

The Owen Jones story suggests that it is worth looking more closely at the opportunities that Port Talbot with its population of 40,000 offered to working-class boys interested in acting between the wars. Central to his development and that of the world-famous actor Richard Burton (who would play Hamlet in his triumphant Old Vic season of 1953–4) was the grammar school and a mentor.

Those fortunate enough to win a place *and* stay on at a grammar school in a Welsh industrial town in the inter-war years were in a privileged and precarious position. They were privileged in that the legacy of late nineteenth-century

educational legislation for Wales was a greater link between elementary and secondary education than in England and a more democratic system, with merit scoring over money in securing secondary school places and a higher percentage of pupils winning free secondary education. Admittedly, as late as 1930 only 5 per cent of the Welsh population over fifteen received any full-time education but the Depression had an unexpected beneficial effect on schooling in Wales. With many families leaving in search of work elsewhere and the consequent decline in the school population, by 1931 10 per cent more elementary school pupils in the 11–12 age bracket in Wales had the opportunity to progress to secondary school than did their counterparts in England.[32]

Port Talbot's other secondary school was the older County School that dated back to 1896 when it opened with eighty-five pupils. Its formal name was the Port Talbot Intermediate School and it was one of the first secondary schools of its kind in Wales. Grammar school pupils from working-class families were in a precarious position since the tough economic conditions of the time – especially for those from mining communities – combined with the school-leaving age of fourteen, made it tempting for parents to opt for the wage that employment could offer rather than keeping their offspring at school. In the years 1931 to 1934, unemployment in Port Talbot stood at an average of 46 per cent.[33]

The steel industry, established in the town in 1901–2,[34] was in the doldrums and blast furnaces were working at half capacity. From 1924 to the end of 1930 only one of the two furnaces at Margam was in blast. Steel production was virtually at a standstill for most of 1927. This, the decline of the tinplate trade and the closure of mines in the lower Afan Valley, saw it classified as a Deprived Area.

Richard Jenkins' eldest sister Cecilia, twenty years his senior (and known as Cis – Sis to Richard), and her husband Elfed James

faced a dilemma early in the war. The newly married couple had taken in the two-year-old Richard[35] to live with them in Taibach in 1927 when his mother Edith Jenkins (née Thomas) had died from septicaemia after the birth of her thirteenth child. Richard's collier father was an alcoholic unable to take care of himself, let alone his younger children, though he worked on and off until he was seventy-five. Richard would visit him and his brothers and sisters and he would sometimes stay in Taibach. Diminutive and toothless, he is remembered as always smiling.

Now Cis and Elfed had two growing children of their own. Elfed (who was not only Richard's brother-in-law but also his second cousin on his mother's side) was a collier but out of work and Richard was a strong lad, old enough to leave school and bring home vital money like most of his contemporaries in Taibach.

Richard had won his all-important scholarship to the Sec in 1937.[36] His success owed a lot to his preparation at the local elementary school, the Eastern Council Schools, originally the Copper Works School. He had progressed from Eastern Infants (where he initially found it difficult to follow lessons in the English language) to Eastern Boys' School. His first teacher there remembered him as having 'wide-awake, big eyes, cow's lick of hair' and freckles, and that he was a voracious reader.[37] His scholarship teacher was the inspiring Meredith Jones, one of a remarkable set of men dedicated to developing in their charges a lifelong interest in the arts.

In 1956 Richard was invited to contribute to a *Sunday Times* series called 'A Turning-Point in Life'.[38] He chose Jones as his catalyst, arguing that he probably would not have become an actor had it not been for this teacher who prepared him for his scholarship. Richard was one of ten boys fortunate enough to pass that year. Jones instilled a thirst for learning into his young charges through engaging them in conversation. He later became a county youth organiser.

The actor's ability as a raconteur surely owed something to Meredith Jones. But it was more than this. He helped Richard to appreciate the beauty of language, to see, for example, that the Twenty-Third Psalm was 'a work of art'. The actor later described this teacher from Cwmafan as 'the concentrated essence of a kind of bi-lingual South Walian', who spoke the alien English 'with a loving care and octosyllabically too!' He was one of those men 'of brilliantly active vocabularies who love an audience'.[39] Richard's first language was Welsh (that Twenty-Third Psalm was most powerful, he maintained, in Welsh). He spoke Welsh at home in Taibach and when in Pontrhydyfen, and it was the language of chapel, though he also spoke English with Elfed James and friends. It was the language of the Sec though Richard studied Welsh as a school subject. Like Meredith Jones, Richard had the heightened awareness that comes with savouring a second language and his teacher taught him to appreciate this.

The Sec provided a good all-round curriculum and promoted a strong sense of belonging to a privileged group of about 300 pupils. Peter Stead has claimed that Welsh grammar school pupils at this time received an education that would 'in a later era be perfectly acceptable at undergraduate level within an American state university'.[40] Crucial to the success of these schools were dedicated teachers. Many of the teachers in Wales were not only intellectuals but also the first in their own families to work in non-manual occupations. The headmaster Christopher Reynolds, who taught mathematics and art, had begun his working life as a north Wales slate quarryman. But it was the appointment in 1925, two months before the birth of Richard Jenkins, of a collier's son from Mountain Ash that was to have the greatest impact.

Philip Henry Burton had been born in 1904. His father died in a mining accident when he was a teenager. He later confided to the Welsh writer Rhys Davies that from the age of fifteen (in

some accounts it was fourteen) he had to 'bear the burden of a widowed and ageing mother, and that permanently crippled me in more ways than one.'[41] After attending Mountain Ash Intermediate School, he won a scholarship aged sixteen to read Pure Mathematics and History at the University College of South Wales and Monmouthshire (forerunner of Cardiff University). Richard Dowling, his supportive headmaster, provided a bank-loan guarantee. Burton got a an Upper-Second Honours degree in History but a Third in Mathematics. However, it was drama – fuelled initially by Mountain Ash's two live theatres and cinema – that was Philip Burton's real passion. The need for a regular job, however, meant that, he became an untrained schoolteacher.

Years later Burton told Hubert Davies (a former pupil who became a primary head teacher in Port Talbot) that he had heard that the Sec wanted somebody to teach Mathematics and start a Latin department.[42] Reckoning that not many would have the requisite qualifications, he applied and was accepted. He also had to teach games. Fortunately Horace James soon took over Latin but Burton taught Maths for ten years. He also began teaching English. For his second decade at the Sec he ran the English department.

Although he had no formal training in the subject, it had, he told Davies, 'become my all-absorbing private study'. He would become a world authority on Shakespeare, write more than a hundred radio scripts and some historical fiction as well as being a BBC drama producer, the Chief Instructor in the BBC Training Department then the director (and first president) of the American Musical and Dramatic Academy in New York.

Port Talbot benefitted enormously from having this talented teacher. Burton operated on a number of levels. He ran a school drama club with weekly meetings. In 1933, for example, members listened to records of John Gielgud's speeches and Burton set up a competition for writing one-act plays and gave

a talk on how to do this.[43] Those Sec pupils who were not deemed School Certificate material were in a class known as 'The Remove'. Burton was given a free hand to work with them and let them produce, design and act in their own modern-dress production of *As You Like It*. The result was, in Burton's own words, 'quite astonishing' and they gave several public performances.[44]

Those displaying more academic promise participated in plays that were well prepared and imaginative. Costumes hired from London arrived by train in a large hamper. When Burton began at the school in 1925 the format was two short plays performed with an entr'acte (a popular pierrot show). But in his third year he put on *A Midsummer Night's Dream*. So began what became the tradition: polished annual productions of challenging plays. Shavian and Shakespearean dramas were favoured and much talked about in the town. Plays were performed in the old school hall. The woodwork master would erect a stage each year especially for them.

Burton's classes were not restricted to school. The Workers' Educational Association (WEA) was flourishing in Port Talbot with its evening classes and day schools. A government report in 1927 noted that the WEA movement in Wales was 'quickly grasping the community as a whole and is assuming the character of a national movement of enlightenment'.[45] In a remarkable scheme the National Library of Wales supplied every WEA class in Wales with a box containing more than two dozen books. Burton ran a WEA class in Modern European History for two seasons then switched to modern drama.[46] University extra-mural classes were held in two-hour weekly sessions and there were weekend schools before and throughout the war. An extra-mural literature class in 1945 studied Spenser, Bacon, Marlowe and Donne as well as Shakespeare.[47]

The town had long had an association with theatre and performance. In the late nineteenth century, Port Talbot, like

other communities in south Wales, received regular visits from showmen with portable theatres (large rectangular tarpaulin tents complete with stage, gallery, seating and heating) popularly known as the 'threepenny gaff'. The main pitches (often for a month) were at Aberafan Cattle Market in Water Street and Taibach Market Place. Here melodramas, farces and tableaux vivants were devoured.[48] They included Edward Ebley's Travelling Theatre. His son worked with a bioscope (travelling cinema) in the early years of the twentieth century. During the First World War Blanche Ebley ran the business whilst her husband and son worked as miners. Ebley Junior and his son then settled in Cwmafan and built a small cinema, which was later re-built and enlarged as the Olympic.[49] In the inter-war years Graham Jenkins, Richard Jenkins' little brother, sang solos there with the Afan Glee Singers.

Leon Vint had built a Palace of Varieties in Water Street Aberavon pre-war, then in 1921 opened the New Theatre in Talbot Road, seating 500. In the thirties it was reinvented as the Empire cinema and brought professional actors to the town. It also hosted an annual visit from a Shakespearean company that provided different plays nightly for a week.

Amateur drama flourished. In 1938 a local newspaper began a weekly column called 'Footlights' about 'Local Dramatics with the Lid off!' It sparked lively debates and correspondence and drew attention to various locations where aspiring thespians could perform. One such hub was the YMCA where Philip Burton had founded a dramatic society.[50] Although Burton's autobiography suggests that this was a real innovation, the town's YMCA dated back to 1898 and an earlier YMCA group had performed *The Merchant of Venice* at the Grand Theatre in Aberavon before the First World War.[51] Another schoolmaster, W. Ivor Nicholas (who had acted in this production), ran a dramatic society for former pupils of the County School.

Nicholas worked with Philip Burton in the YMCA drama

society. Its success helped to keep the place solvent. Burton took the lead in most of their plays. Their first production was T. W. Robertson's *Caste*, after which they moved on to Dickens, Shaw and Shakespeare (Burton's performance as Othello for the YMCA at the Cross Hands Drama Festival won a silver cup). They were based in several huts near the railway station.[52] However, in April 1940, Burton, their chairman, opened a purpose-built YMCA in Talbot Road. This YMCA, closer to Richard's home, was soon the largest in Wales.[53]

The development of a national movement for physical fitness saw the National Fitness Council provide more than half of the £9,500 it cost to build and equip. Steel companies and donations from individuals supplied the rest. The YMCA could now cater for more than 600 young men and boys. Young men 'of good character' over the age of sixteen paid 7/6d yearly or 2d a week (this could be deducted from wages for steelworkers). Facilities included table tennis, billiards, a lounge, workshop, gym and a Boys' Club room. Richard turned fifteen in November and joined the YMCA the following month.

There was also a chapel, since the YMCA was part of a worldwide movement for Christian young men that boasted almost 11,000 branches and aimed to link 'spiritual enrichment, educational improvement, physical recreation and social relaxation'.[54] A team of voluntary helpers ran a Forces Canteen. Most importantly for its dramatic society, a hall seated 350. There was a host of clubs and societies and a Ladies Auxiliary, although the emphasis here, as in other social activities, was primarily on boys and those serving in the forces.[55]

No time was wasted in putting on drama at the new YMCA. The week-long festivities celebrating the spring opening culminated in the YMCA dramatic society presenting *White Collar*, written and produced by Burton.[56] The character of Uncle Jim in his *Granton Street* (first performed at the old YMCA in 1934) had been so popular that he wrote this sequel.

But it was another cultural event that prompted his extensive connections with the BBC and so provided the opportunity for his more promising pupils to glimpse a wider world. Margam Abbey had been founded in 1147, and in 1937 its anniversary was celebrated in the form of a pageant unfolding the abbey's rich history. Burton was asked to write and direct it. It was an amateur production, researched by the Sec's History Master with a cast of hundreds of local people. A member of the Talbot family played the part of the Virgin Mary in the final dramatic scene and the crowd sang a hymn to her.

Attending the final performance was T. Rowland Hughes, features producer for the BBC in Wales, another son of a north Wales quarryman. He asked Burton to write a version for the radio. At first Burton protested that it was too visual for radio but was persuaded to persist. Three more radio scripts (about Shakespeare) followed. This same year saw the establishment of a distinct Welsh Region of the BBC with its own wavelength. From 1937 onwards – interrupted by a scholarship tour of the United States just before the outbreak of war – Burton divided his time between teaching and writing plays for the BBC. Port Talbot's easy access to Cardiff made this possible for the Sec's Senior Master.

The school was in an advantageous position. In May 1942 Hughes and Burton worked on a radio production of *How Green Was My Valley*. A number of scenes were recorded at the Sec (some in the playground). Burton played the schoolmaster Mr Jonas and thirteen-year-old Hubert Clements from Aberafan was the young Huw Morgan. Hubert Davies of Taibach had another leading role. The local paper commented pointedly on the advantage of genuine Welsh accents. The previous autumn had seen the release of the film of Richard Llewellyn's novel. Shot in California at the Fox Ranch at Malibu Canyon, it had used just one Welsh actor (and in a minor role).[57]

Former Sec pupils acknowledge the quality of the teaching they received. Graham Hughes, who became a law professor at

New York University, recalled the 'magnificent instruction' he enjoyed in English, Latin and French and described his education in the war years as 'the most concentrated, formative and enriching of my life'.[58] He received two years of Greek tuition from the Latin master even though Greek wasn't on the curriculum. Burton gave up 'some of his very scant free time' to tutor Hughes for his Cambridge scholarship.

Above all, it was the magic of Burton's lessons that is recalled by surviving ex-pupils. Rosalie Mahoney (née Trussler), who lives in Missouri – she married one of the GIs stationed in Porthcawl – attended the Sec between 1936 and 1940. She remembers Burton's 'marvellous voice' and how he adopted different voices for the various characters when reading Shakespeare to the class. Then there were his words of wisdom: she recalls Burton telling them 'if you haven't read the Bible twice, you're not educated... none of us had... but that's what he said'.[59] The poet Ruth Bidgood (née Jones) was the daughter of the vicar of St Mary's Aberavon and became a prefect. She too appreciates Burton's skills. She studied English at Oxford University, dedicated her first volume of poetry *The Given Time* (1972) to her former teacher and became a friend of his.

Simeon Jones, who would later teach for a year at the school and become deputy head teacher at Glan Afan (the former County School), acted in Burton's plays when a schoolboy. He saw how the teacher would 'wrestle out the quality he wanted' once he had spotted a potential talent. After acting in Bernard Shaw's *Saint Joan* in 1938, he and Eifion Davies (who became a headmaster) were whisked off to Cardiff by car with Burton – still in their stage make-up – for the experience of visiting Broadcasting House. Burton also addressed the school's Forum Society on how the play should be seen as a dramatic plea for toleration.[60] The Welsh regional director of the BBC, R. Hopkin Morris, gave the inaugural address to this society in 1937.

Burton's love of literature was inspirational, as Hubert Davies

recalls, and his personality 'almost magnetic'. So absorbed was the teacher in drama that pupils spent a disproportionate amount of time studying Shakespeare with far less attention paid to grammar and the curriculum for matriculation. But it still paid dividends in exam results and in pupils' lifelong appreciation of drama.

Burton had recognised that the eleven-year-old Hubert Davies had a good speaking voice and he was permitted two days off school weekly for six weeks whilst he took part in a *Children's Hour* BBC radio serial in Cardiff. Burton wanted to adopt him too, but the child's father refused. Davies became a teacher and preacher and remained active in amateur dramatics.

Philip Burton's dedication to the handsome Richard Jenkins has recently been the cause of some speculation.[61] His wish to adopt several promising schoolboys over the years raises eyebrows today but, as we shall see in relation to Richard Jenkins, Burton's behaviour needs to be understood in the context of a very different society and a total commitment to providing opportunities through drama.

It was during a trip to Cardiff with Burton that the youth who would become Richard Burton saw his first professional play. Years later he claimed that when asked what he had thought of it, he had been non-committal about the acting but keen on the applause.[62] This may well be an example of his ability to craft his life story retrospectively. He was not only a superb storyteller intoxicated by the richness of the English language, but also understandably critical of misleading early biographies that were, as he put it, 'agog with sensationalism', and therefore keen to supply his own account.[63]

It was on 6 February 1940 that the fourteen-year-old Richard Jenkins first mentioned Philip Burton in the pocket diary he had started a couple of months earlier: 'Had a fine afternoon especially with Burton who talked about Astronomy'.[64] The teacher and studying would soon feature more regularly. It was,

however, playing rugby and going to the cinema that became Richard's twin passions. He was a very competent wing forward. Just before his fifteenth birthday he became captain of the house team. He was in the school rugby team even though it contained boys two years older than him. International matches were suspended during the war but a former chair of the Welsh Secondary Schools Rugby Union listed Richard Jenkins[65] as one of the young players who would otherwise have been a serious contender.

Richard played for the town's junior team at Aberavon Rugby Football Club's Athletic Ground on Saturday mornings. He captained the under-14s. This was after his newspaper round and delivering old newspapers to the fish and chip shop (as well as eyeing potatoes). Like many local boys he earned cash by doing a number of odd jobs such as collecting manure from the mountain and selling it.

Saturday afternoons during the rugby season were spent with Elfed James and James' father watching the senior Aberavon team known as The Wizards. When the club celebrated its centenary in 1976 Richard wrote an article for their booklet in which he recalled the thrill of following home games and how he had longed to become an Aberavon player. He was in the school's junior cricket team, played tennis at the Memorial Park and, like many in Taibach, enjoyed boxing. On the eve of the First World War the village had produced a British bantamweight champion called Billy Beynon. Richard boxed as an amateur at the YMCA and twice fought for cash.[66]

He could frequently be found at one of Taibach's two cinemas, the new Regent and the Picturedrome (originally the Workers' Hall) known as The Cach.[67] In one year (from November 1939) he saw on average a film a week, attendance aided by the free passes the Picturedrome gave to the local barber who passed them on to a friend of Richard's who had a part-time job sweeping up after haircuts. In the centre of town

was the Forge Road Electric Cinema. Although its days were numbered, it would have a belated moment of glory in the late forties when, bizarrely, it was hired out for use as a film set. *Blue Scar* (1949), with a rare female director (Jill Craigie), explored the background to nationalisation via a mining family. The film was shot locally in the mining village of Abergwynfi and in the Electric, now filled with coal and transformed into a coal mine.[68]

One of the many films that Richard devoured was Alexander Korda's *The Four Feathers* starring Ralph Richardson. Owen Jones had secured a part in this film but had to relinquish it as he was contracted to a repertory theatre. The film was loosely based on an Edwardian novel and set in 1898, with British soldiers sent to the Sudan to avenge the earlier death of the imperial hero General Gordon. Many years later, in 2002, Michael Sheen appeared in another version of this story focusing on a British army officer (played by Heath Ledger) accused of cowardice before redeeming himself in an expedition to rescue Gordon.

The town's love affair with the big screen can be observed by looking at the *Port Talbot Guardian*. An advertisement for the Majestic Cinema (which Richard occasionally visited) might take up half a page. In 1940 the impending opening of the Plaza, 'Port Talbot's New Luxury Super-Cinema' commandeered an entire page.[69] Lists of the times of showings, pictures of film stars, accounts of 'Next Week's Amusements' and serialised synopses (syndicated by arrangement with Metro-Goldwyn-Mayer) took up more space than did accounts of Hitler. They supplied a vital escape valve in wartime. Meanwhile, at the Wesley Hall, Bert Richards of the Midland Bank entertained children with film shows that encompassed Charlie Chaplin comedies, cowboy shows and Dickensian stories.[70]

Graham Jenkins, who sometimes accompanied his brother to the cinema, has observed that Richard's early, somewhat

declamatory, acting style owed something to the films he watched. The oratory and *hwyl* of the pulpit also had an impact. In August 1940 Richard's diary recorded him getting the autograph of a good new preacher in his chapel. Richard was steeped in a chapel culture that included recitation. This provided a number of valuable skills, including an early training in memorising and performing in front of an audience.

His niece, the actor Siân Owen, has stressed that her first platform was the chapel and that 'Having to stand in front of everybody on a Sunday morning and say your verse' instilled confidence from a young age and was a huge advantage. Richard's diary shows him attending Noddfa Welsh Congregational Chapel.[71] The James family went three times on Sundays and Elfed James' father was a Deacon, so Richard's entries sometimes mention entire days spent in chapel.

He often returned to Pontrhydyfen at weekends and his sister Hilda Owen has recalled how he used to re-enact the Welsh prayers and sermons of the preacher he had just listened to, inserting extra flourishes and drama and delighting in his captive audience of sisters. On Sunday 10 November 1940 it was his fifteenth birthday, yet in his diary entry for that day he makes no mention of this, instead writing, 'It seemed that the chapel had about £31 last Sunday which is not bad at all for a small chapel'.[72] Even after he moved to live at Burton's lodgings, Richard attended chapel on Sundays with his family. In the 1960s he described the pulpit as the world's greatest stage with the great preachers as the stars of his youth.[73]

In 1943 Richard won joint first place in the inter-house Scripture Reading competition in the school Eisteddfod. He also had a decent singing voice. He got third prize for his boy's solo in the county Youth Eisteddfod at Bridgend in 1943.[74] But his singing was not as good as that of his younger brother who, at one stage, had a regular slot on the radio as a 'Boy Warbler'. Graham Jenkins' soprano voice won him prizes at various

Eisteddfodau. But when they were pitted against each other Richard was the one with the confidence and competitive edge to beat his brother for the singing prize.[75]

During these years Richard became a voracious reader. He and many others were fortunate in that Taibach boasted the town's Central Library, which had been built as a free circulating library during the First World War with a grant from the Carnegie Trust. It had an enlightened and helpful librarian in David T. Eaton, who encouraged many an autodidact. Eaton also became secretary of the local branch of the WEA and was a noted eisteddfodwr.[76] Graham Jenkins claims that the library was his brother's 'favourite retreat' in Taibach.[77] Richard's love of books was to last for the rest of his life and, as Stead has discerned, his cultural compass was set during his formative years in Port Talbot and essentially framed by his grammar school experience.[78] Chris Williams, editor of *The Richard Burton Diaries*, has recently presented a lesser-known side of the actor: as a keen reader of literature, history and politics, a critic and aspirant scholar.[79]

This is something I can vouch for too. He read my MA dissertation (on the Chartist endurance in Merthyr Tydfil between 1840–68) one evening and then carefully quizzed me on it the following day. I recall him devouring books such as a huge tome on the Third Reich. We discussed fiction and politics and (fuelled some of – but by no means all of – the time by vodka) he would quote liberally from the poetry of R. S. Thomas, W. B. Yeats and many others.

The young Richard Jenkins had recorded in October 1940 that he was reading on average about three books in two days. Although diaries need to be treated with caution – they are, after all, known as 'ego documents' and this diarist was always a good spinner of stories – his comment is interesting. Even though this was probably an exaggeration, it suggests that he valued reading and wanted to comment on his prowess. The

very fact that a lad of fourteen had been sufficiently disciplined to write an articulate and daily diary for more than a year is itself worth noting.

Written initially in pencil then inked over, he usually filled the seven lines allotted daily. His spelling, with a few exceptions such as 'apsus' and 'refferring', was good. There were several misuses of prepositions (for example, 'Am listening of the news now') but his grammar and writing were remarkably accomplished for someone of his age and for whom English had not been his first language. In amongst daily accounts of work, play and scraping together money for the cinema are sentences such as: 'I am writing this in the cold hours of Thursday morning'.[80] He provides comments on the war both internationally and at home as well as personal remarks on his social life and education. The entries (see Illustration 7) suggest too how much his schooling mattered.

That same year Humphrey Lyttleton was writing a diary in Port Talbot.[81] The future jazz musician and broadcaster had just left Eton College where he had been born as well as educated – his father was a housemaster – and was filling in time before enlisting in the Grenadier Guards. His uncle and godfather, Richard Lyttleton, was a steel executive (he became president of the British Iron and Steel Federation) and had obtained jobs for Lyttleton and his cousin Anthony in the steelworks. Labouring at the coke ovens and marathon drinking sessions at the Working Men's Club in Velindre introduced the young gentlemen to a novel world. In his diary Lyttleton admitted that Port Talbot seemed like a foreign land. Eighteen months later he was taking his commission at Sandhurst.

In February 1941 the centre of Swansea was destroyed in the 'Three Nights Blitz'. Port Talbot was comparatively fortunate but did not escape completely. The young Ivor Emmanuel, who would make his name in musical entertainment on the stage as well as in film and television, lost his parents, his younger sister

Mair and grandfather when a bomb hit his home in Morgan's Terrace, Pontrhydyfen.[82] A barrage balloon fell and burned for a time in Richard's street in Taibach. But unfortunately we have no extant diary from him for 1941.

By the end of that year more than 150 Old Boys were serving in the forces. Old Girls were joining the Women's Auxiliary Air Force and National Fire Service. The *Wayfarer* (the school magazine) reported former pupils who were killed, missing or wounded on active service across the world. By 1945 the Roll of Honour had 30 names. Teachers left to serve in the Forces, and classes in some subjects were shared between the Sec and the County School. Pupils had to carry gas masks, and lessons were interrupted by air raid warnings and retreats to shelters. School meals were rationed. Exercise books were in such short supply that a return to slates was mooted but rejected. Few chemicals were available for laboratory work. The school year was affected: hours were shortened for some months so in 1940 the summer holiday lasted for a meagre three weeks.[83]

Richard Jenkins had made his first appearance on stage early in 1941. It was not, however, a great success. It was in Bernard Shaw's play *The Apple Cart* directed by Philip Burton and was one of the first amateur productions of the play in Britain.[84] Richard had just a small part as the American Ambassador in London but was 'resplendent in top coat, stars and stripes jacket and blue trousers'.[85] The play was put on at the YMCA rather than the school hall (dictated by blackout restrictions). Burton later admitted to having 'no recollection' of Richard's performance.[86] At the time he told him that he sounded more like a gangster than an educated American. Clearly the teenager had not heeded the advice Burton had given several years earlier when he had urged pupils to 'be critical and discriminating in the choice of films they saw'.[87]

Richard also became involved in drama at the new Taibach County Youth Centre established in 1941 by the Glamorgan

Education Authority at his old Eastern Schools. It formed one of just three such experimental centres created at this time. It is no coincidence that the county councillor Llewellyn Heycock (who in 1967 would become Lord Heycock of Taibach) was behind this and became its president. He would be instrumental in the development of the county's educational opportunities and Port Talbot's early championship of comprehensive education, as well as chairing the education authority and later the county council. He had also been a pupil at the Eastern Schools.

The Youth Centre was somewhat dingy and draughty but it was open three nights a week for young people aged fourteen to twenty-five. It was a much appreciated and valuable amenity in the midst of war. It earned praise from socialists already familiar with the area, for example the renowned political scientist Professor Harold Laski, who had lectured in Taibach's Gibeon Chapel in 1940. Minnie Pallister, who had composed a song about Ramsay MacDonald's Aberavon election sung to the tune of *Men of Harlech*, also championed it. She addressed the Carnegie Library in 1941 at a meeting organised by the Taibach Co-operative Education Committee.[88] James Griffiths MP visited the club the following year and spoke warmly about its 'adventurous spirit' in the dramatic arts'.[89]

Meredith Jones, Jenkins' former teacher, became the Youth Centre's first Warden, supported by Rose Newman. The local historian and teacher Leslie Evans joined as a young Arts and Crafts Instructor. He has paid tribute to the way in which the 'mercurial and effusive' Jones, assisted by Llewellyn Heycock, 'touched off a cultural spark which has flared through the years in a blaze of multifarious activities'.[90]

Richard Jenkins was a lively, confident lad and, as Evans recalled in the 1980s, one amongst 'a great many eager intelligent youngsters'.[91] Yet although the teenager spent many hours there, the centre's magazine *The Bridge* did not single him

out at this stage as worthy of special attention. This suggests how Richard was perceived at the time rather than in the light of the glamour and greatness that would come to surround him and potentially influence retrospective interpretations.

There were dances and table tennis, billiards and, from the end of 1942, a canteen. When the evening's activities formally ended Jones would extend the opportunity to exercise his verbal gymnastics as the lads accompanied him on his walk home. Richard's descriptions evoke for the modern reader Alan Bennett's play *The History Boys*.[92] The actor recalled how Jones would 'turn all things, from Rugby football to a walk over the Brombil [a beautiful secluded valley in Margam] to T. S. Eliot, into powerful drama in the telling of it'. He suggested Jones' transformational power: 'astonishingly we potential corner-boys and billiard markers would catch a glimpse of the glory of man from Meredith's play with the assumption that two and two makes four'[93]. David Jenkins, Richard's policeman brother has told how his young brother would often arrive home in Caradoc Street after eleven o'clock at night, telling Cis and Elfed James how he had been 'Talking with Mered'.[94]

Leo Lloyd was another inspirational figure. He had a huge impact on Port Talbot's love affair with drama. He was employed in the steelworks as a traffic yardmaster but his passion was producing plays. Born in Barnstaple the son of a Llanelli schoolmaster, he lived in west and south Wales when young and was educated at Bridgend Grammar School. He first become interested in drama when participating in chapel operettas and plays in Bridgend. When working at Blaenavon Iron and Steel Company he formed a dramatic society. He began by acting but was soon producing.

In 1924 he moved to Port Talbot and two years later began a local amateur group, the Thespian Dramatic Society, known as 'The Thespians'. He was put in charge of the Drama Group at the Taibach Youth Centre. It later became Taibach Young People's

Theatre and eventually Taibach People's Theatre. On May Day 1939, Aberavon Divisional Labour Party and local branches of the South Wales Miners' Federation ended their Parade (at which the Labour leader Ben Tillett spoke) with a free performance of Leo Lloyd's production of Walter Greenwood's powerful *Love on the Dole*.[95]

Richard Burton has acknowledged that it was Lloyd who persuaded him that acting was 'infinitely fascinating'. He:

> taught me discipline and he taught me, by inference, and from his devotion to the craft, that 'reality' can be greater *on* the stage than *off*. He channelled my discontent and made me want to be an actor.[96]

That discontent was not just the restlessness of a volatile teenager. Although Richard had been a promising pupil academically (doing especially well in chemistry and geometry exams in 1940), the adverse economic circumstances facing his family and the chance of a job had resulted in him leaving school when he was fifteen and, crucially, before he had the chance to matriculate. He became a draper's assistant in the men's outfitters department of the Taibach Co-operative Central Stores, earning not quite thirty shillings a week.[97] It was tantalisingly situated opposite the Central Library. A fellow employee remembers him reciting Shakespeare when he should have been getting on with his work. Richard, the son of a coal miner[98] and with an *in loco parentis* brother-in-law who was also a collier, found this job emasculating and loathed it. The Youth Centre was a welcome diversion in the evenings.

Thanks to Leo Lloyd, Richard was one of seven members from the Youth Centre's Drama Group – 'exuberant youngsters' – who acted in Glamorgan's first Youth Eisteddfod in June 1942, which was held in Pontypridd Grammar School. He was cast in a leading role as the reformed escaped convict in *The Bishop's*

Candlesticks, a one-act adaptation of Victor Hugo's *Les Misérables*.[99] Ironically, the actor whose voice was to be his greatest asset was denied the chance to speak, as the production was in mime. But Taibach did at least win first prize.

Leslie Evans was suitably impressed and has recalled how Richard's remarkable performance was acclaimed by all present. Although detecting some evidence of Richard's inexperience – he was, after all, only sixteen – he 'commanded the stage and riveted the audience'.[100] He also carried away second prize in the competition for English Reading and third prize for Recitation in English as well as being the runner-up in a singing solo.

Meanwhile, those fortunate enough to have stayed on in school enjoyed various theatrical treats. A London actor (Mr Burke) came to the school to give a dramatic recital and, in the autumn of 1941, Senior pupils were taken to the Gwyn Hall in Neath to see Sybil Thorndike and Lewis Casson perform in Euripedes' *Medea*. Dame Sybil and her husband spent two months touring the south Wales valleys as well as coastal towns (and returned there in 1942).[101] Casson told the play's translator Gilbert Murray that 'The big emotional sway and the beauty of the poetry really do give these Welsh people what they want'.[102] Had he talked to the Sec seniors he might have heard a more critical interpretation. They had already been treated to an introductory talk about the play from the Latin master and although they enjoyed the acting by the professionals, the young people felt that it had been so altered 'in form and setting' that 'much of the effectiveness of Greek drama seemed to have been lost'.[103]

There was a school production of Shakespeare's *Richard II*. Richard had been studying the play for his School Certificate but the former pupil turned Co-op employee could no longer participate. He also missed out on the broadcasting for 'Overseas listeners' of Philip Burton's account of school life in

wartime entitled 'With Satchel and Gas-Mask.' This brought the BBC to the Sec for two days.

Richard did, however, appear as one of nine Port Talbot Squadron cadets in Philip Burton's *Venture, Adventure*. In addition to all his other duties Burton was now Flight Lieutenant of Squadron 499 of the Air Training Corps (ATC) preparing young volunteers for the RAF. The documentary told the story of the ATC and its effects on the youth of south Wales. Richard had joined the town's ATC and did some fire-watching duties with both Burton and David Eaton the librarian, making the most of this opportunity to seek advice and learn from these two intellectuals. Leaving school seems to have sharpened his determination to study and to find some way out of being a shop assistant.

H. G. Wells had also been a draper's assistant. He worked at Southsea Drapery Emporium, aged fourteen, as an apprentice. He had hated his incarceration and been intensely unhappy but put the experience to good use, publishing his novel *Kipps* in 1905. It was about a draper's assistant who inherits a fortune.

Richard too got his break but in an unexpected form. Meredith Jones discovered that, for some months, the teenager had been unwillingly wielding tape measures, coupons and yards of cloth. Jones managed, with vital help from Llewellyn Heycock (a school governor, member of the county council and neighbour of Richard's), to get his former pupil reinstated at the Sec. Such networking – almost like the plot for a play – says much about the local community at a time when war was putting untold pressures on daily life. Many years later the immensely rich actor told Graham Jenkins that the letter inviting him back to school as a scholarship pupil was the most valuable offer he ever received.

Reflecting on the autumn term of 1942, the House Notes for the school magazine recorded that 'We would like to take this opportunity of welcoming back Richard Jenkins to our ranks.

For in the past he has proved a valuable member of the House [Leisan[104]], and we are sure he will be so in the future.'[105] Philip Burton was the House Master and no ordinary one, for the Home Service now regularly broadcast his work from London. In *Miss Bradley*, for example, Diana Wynyard played the title role in a play about a female Mr Chips. He was also producing programmes and writing wartime features such as *Plyber the Fisherman*, about Breton resistance to Nazi tyranny and *The Pride of Britain*, commissioned to commemorate the second anniversary of Dunkirk.[106]

That October in Hollywood M.G.M. signed the ten-year-old Elizabeth Taylor for the film *Lassie Come Home*. The following month Richard had a decent role in a play staged by Burton. This was in Ronald Gow's *Gallows Glorious*. Its hero was the American abolitionist John Brown and Richard played his son Owen. Brinley Jenkins from Cwmafan (not a relative) had the leading part. He also came first in the 'keenly contested' annual St David's Day Eisteddfod's dramatic recitation the following spring, beating Richard Jenkins into second place.[107]

A surviving copy of the programme for *Gallows Glorious* includes the signatures of the cast. This suggests the change in Richard's fortunes. Brinley Jenkins' signature is in a small neat hand at the top of the page. But the name that is positioned just above the play's title in the centre, signed with confidence and commanding attention, is that of Richard Jenkins.[108] The school magazine reported that he gave an assured performance that culminated in 'sustaining the powerful climax with fine effect'.[109]

The returning pupil had diplomatically suggested that he wanted to become a teacher. This was the ambition of many a working-class youth seeking a secure professional life. Vivian Allen, who had won plaudits for his part as the English chaplain in Burton's school production of *Saint Joan*, and the promising Simeon Jones were two such boys singled out by Burton for

coaching for the stage but who both then opted to train as teachers. Burton also coached Evan Morgan and was keen for him to go to RADA but his parents too envisaged their son as a teacher.[110] As one of the characters in Philip Burton's play *White Collar* (1938) comments: 'In Wales teaching seems to be the destiny of most of the pupils who are lucky enough to get through the examination and then lucky enough to get a place in College'.[111]

Decades later Richard mused in his diary about another boy, Morgan Griffiths, 'who seemed to us all at the time to be a god-given actor', with his mellifluous voice and air of authority in the school plays.[112] After a lifetime of working with actors on both sides of the Atlantic, Philip Burton remained 'convinced that the proportion of acting talent in that school was higher than in any comparable group I have met since'. He was 'amazed' by the 'amount of genuine talent that was unearthed' and the 'quite extraordinary performances' of these youngsters.[113]

He did have high standards. Brinley Jenkins detected something of the martinet there.[114] But the dedication of these young people was remarkable. Simeon Jones has recalled playing tough rugby matches with Richard and the rest of the team. In the showers afterwards they would, of their own volition, quote lines from Shakespeare. Someone would start, for example, 'So foul and fair a day I have not seen' and another would take up – word perfect – the lines from *Macbeth*.

Philip Burton briefly wondered whether the political conscience that Richard seemed to be developing might mean devoting his life to the Labour Party.[115] The town had, after all, a proud Labour tradition. Aberavon had returned Ramsay MacDonald as its Member of Parliament just before he became Britain's first Labour Prime Minister. Richard was even related (his father was a first cousin) to Sir William Jenkins, the distinguished Labour MP for the adjoining constituency of

Neath. The son of a coalminer, William Jenkins had been a railway worker and collier, sat on the executive of the South Wales Miners' Federation and in 1922 became Chief Agent for the Afan Valley Miners' Association. He chaired Glamorgan County Council after the First World War (Richard discovered that certificates for county youth Eisteddfodau came rubber-marked with his relative's signature) and later the Federation of Education Authorities for Wales. He was first elected Neath's MP in 1922, a position he held until his death in 1944.[116] Richard joined the Labour Party and later described himself as an 'emotional Socialist'.[117]

His lack of deference and the need to do well after being given a rare second chance to study must have put him in an awkward position at the Sec. It would have been difficult returning to the status of a schoolboy and years later he described himself as having been 'a rough, tough boy who took a bit of handling'.[118] He was also finding life restrictive at home in Caradoc Street and there was increasing tension between him and Elfed James. It cannot have been easy for either of them. When a room became vacant at Philip Burton's lodgings in Connaught Street in the spring of 1943, Richard moved in and thus provided an opportunity for the teacher to train and hone the acting skills of this promising teenager along the lines that he most valued.

Richard Jenkins may not have attended drama school but he had instead a privileged, intensive and sustained one-to-one tuition. Both tutor and student now shared an ambition and determination for him to succeed. Nevertheless, Philip Burton later stressed that he would never advise anyone to take up an acting career as it was 'so precarious and heartbreaking'. He admitted that 'Even Richard's decision was very much his own', though 'of course, once he had made it, I was with him the whole way'.[119] Richard's dedication is especially remarkable given his low boredom threshold. Yet his diary writing from a young age suggests that he possessed an ability to persevere

with what he perceived to be valuable as well as an appreciation of literature and language.

Peter Stead has commented on the unfortunate timing of Richard's training, arguing that his chance to prove himself came at a moment when the English theatre was emerging from a memorable era.[120] Owen Jones had glimpsed its power only to have it snatched away. The war had altered aspirations and the focus of the theatre. Now, along with the burgeoning film industry, it had new agendas and ambitions that did not fully accord with the classical training provided by his mentor. It might even be claimed that the young man was being prepared for an obsolescent world of theatre. But without the benefit of hindsight and with what he discerned as a real talent, Philip Burton did what he could and that was a lot.

One summer holiday he took Richard to Stratford-on-Avon. The plays they saw included *Dr Faustus*. Years later Richard Burton would act in *Faustus* with Oxford students and make a film of Marlowe's play. Now he and Philip Burton spent their afternoons working on the play's final soliloquy on the lawn at the back of their guesthouse.[121]

It is tempting to ask what the other guests thought of this man in his late thirties on holiday with a sixteen-year-old schoolboy. Today the fact that Richard moved to his teacher's digs also seems remarkable. After the war he shared a flat in Cardiff with Philip Burton. Had one of the very promising schoolgirls at the Sec – for example Anita Davies who was a much acclaimed Saint Joan or Dilys Jones who played Eliza Doolittle in *Pygmalion* with Richard – gone up the mountain with Mr Burton to project the voice, many tongues would have wagged.

Burton's autobiography *Early Doors* suggests a familiarity between himself and the schoolboy who would take his name. For example he refers to Richard as 'seizing every opportunity of *our private life* [my emphasis] to assuage his thirst for

knowledge'. The writings of Burton's later years are less guarded than his earlier comments. The title of his 1992 book *Richard & Philip: The Burtons* is deliberately familiar, playing with the renowned pairing of Richard Burton and Elizabeth Taylor. It could afford to be less circumspect since it was published eight years after Richard's death.[122]

In the early 1940s Philip Burton was, however, living in a society that was markedly different from that of his later years in Florida's Key West. He was known as a bookish intellectual, respected by his landlady and her daughters. Described in the local press as difficult to approach, with 'Teutonic appearance; Schubert-like visage', he was presented as an example of rectitude and moderation (he neither smoked nor drank).[123] He would have been only too well aware that Richard was adamantly heterosexual – already a big hit with the town's young women. Rona McQue, a Swansea University student, was on teaching practice at the school (teaching French) and remembers how Richie Jenkins 'used to knock the staffroom door very politely. He was a handsome looking lad and the young teachers would swoon'. And she was impressed by the presence and status of Mr Burton.

Any overtures from Burton towards Richard could well have prompted aggression from him, put an end to the whole 'experiment' and seen the schoolmaster charged with breaking a law that was not reformed until 1967 (and Richard was still a minor). So Burton's championing of the undeniably attractive and dedicated student would have been conducted in a manner that was without reproach. Any one-sided passion would have been sublimated into turning raw and eager talent into an actor for the future.

It was thought imperative at this time to iron out strong accents in order to succeed on the English stage or in the BBC for anything other than plays set in specific regional locations. Owen Jones' relatives have recalled the 'upper crust' English

accent he assumed in a radio play they heard in the 1930s, doubtless the result of Burton's training.[124] For his own debut BBC radio play about Shakespeare's life, Burton had been allowed to use three of the Sec's pupils as actors, provided they sounded English. Alban Cochlin, who played the young Shakespeare, later recalled 'the heart-breaking gruelling which had been necessary – yes! Very necessary' to wipe out his strong Welsh accent so that he spoke 'for the time being at least, respectable English'.[125] Richard had, at this point, been in his first year at the school and could not have been mistaken for an English boy. He had attended the auditions but had not been chosen.

Now, five years later, Richard was subjected to a rigorous regime to anglicise his voice, although his tutor, already familiar with the United States, sought a mid-Atlantic accent. A teacher who revered English literature and language, had English parents and learned literary Welsh was working with an adolescent whose first language was Welsh but who studied through the medium of English. Together they produced a remarkable symbiosis: a classical actor who would, in time, be perceived by many as Olivier's heir. Yet ultimately it was Richard Burton's retention of a Welsh dimension to that voice – most evidenced in his reading of the work of Dylan Thomas – that made him distinctive.[126] The BBC studio manager for the renowned radio recording of *Under Milk Wood* has recently recalled the impact of hearing him perform: 'His voice was so sonorous and beautiful you felt something shift in the air around you'.[127]

Richard was trained in the front room of Mrs Smith's digs for long hours daily after school. Up on Mynydd Margam (Margam Mountain) he was taught to project his voice by reciting Shakespeare, encouraged to value distinctness rather than volume and shown how to shape vowels, creating what Stead has called his 'ecclesiastical voice'.[128] This voice became, as

Burton put it, 'memorably beautiful'.[129] He also found Richard to be a 'relentless questioner'[130] with a remarkable ability to retain the poetry and prose he learned. He was taught how to cultivate a stage presence and a grace in movement.

This training was about more than shaping an actor. Philip Burton's own story was one of social mobility through education and the making of Richard Burton suggests the teacher's wish to pass this on to the next generation. In 1934, aged thirty, Burton had published *Granton Street*, the first of two plays set in Abernansant, a fictitious Glamorgan mining town.[131] The play opens on the eve of a by-election and we are in the Davies family's front room (where the entire action takes place: the play had been written as a challenge to produce a credible three-act play in one setting). They are stalwart Labour supporters. The father sits on the lodge committee of the South Wales Miners' Federation and the eldest son is a 'hothead' increasingly impatient with cautious methods. John Davies, the younger son, who has trained to be a doctor, returns to his old home. There is some social awkwardness during the meal as the young professional offers his sister a plate before helping himself and is rebuked by his father: 'We don't stand on ceremony here. We're at home, not in a restaurant.'[132]

John reveals a shocking secret: a determination to marry the daughter of Edward Granton, the Tory candidate. Granton is also the local mine owner and employer. It is a tale of class and class consciousness as well as embourgeoisement. Both the daughter Mary and her uncle suggest ways of envisaging the world that are not entirely bound by capital and labour. This is a play about change and the potential for the future. Uncle Jim, dismissed by most as a drunken layabout, articulates the key arguments. He stresses that there now exists, thanks to the extension of higher education, a new division in society between the cultured and the uncultured: 'The members of this new cultured class are drawn from the ranks of all the old classes'.[133]

In some respects Richard Burton as envisaged by his mentor can be compared with the character of John Davies the deracinated doctor. The strong-minded young woman John wishes to marry is called Sybil. Ironically, so too was the woman who would become Richard's first wife and whose father was a colliery under-manager in the Rhondda. Richard also, of course, represented Philip Burton's own ambitions, although – unlike most instances of the older person fulfilling their thwarted dreams through the younger generation – Phillip Burton's career would continue to develop.

Retrospectively Richard Burton appeared ambivalent about his chosen profession and colluded, as he often did, in myth-making about his life story. Gethin Matthews has commented that 'the best performance Richard Jenkins ever gave was his portrayal of Richard Burton'.[134] Yet although it was said that 'real men' of his time went down the mines rather than on the stage, opting for the profession of acting did make sense for Richard at the time he embraced it.

For a start this was wartime and the delineation of occupations had, for the moment, shed its usual rigidity. Richard had lived through a period when those around him had suffered greatly through losing work. When his brother Verdun began work down the pit two days after his fourteenth birthday in 1930, he was the only one in work in the family and earned a mere 7/6d weekly.[135] But Richard was the second youngest in his large family. Aspirations for the youngest members of the Jenkins clan were different from those of the older siblings and Richard had already been given a second chance.

Boys who had been socialised into valuing literature in school and chose to recite Shakespeare in the showers saw their futures as hopefully involving study of some sort. Richard Jenkins was competitive and assured. He wanted a passport to a world that would take him far from his early job experience and, thanks to Philip Burton's endorsement, commitment and connections,

acting appeared to provide that way out, not least because this was the passion of his teacher. He later claimed that his childhood was dominated by wanting to play for Aberavon and get to Oxford.[136] The latter does not appear to have been apparent at the time but his early diary does demonstrate his desire to study.

Richard Burton's reaction in the 1960s to an early draft of Philip Burton's *Early Doors* is revealing. He wrote[137] an excoriating unpublished review of the memoir (at that stage entitled *Time & Telling*). It reversed the old pupil-teacher relationship, showing Richard as the judge and one especially critical of Burton's style. Richard Burton dismissed the bulk of the book as dull, pretentious and egocentric (though he at least spared Burton from ever seeing his comments). He was especially scathing about the early chapters and uneasy about their focus on the poverty of Philip Burton's youth. The only part of the book Richard Burton liked was the one chapter where Philip Burton was not recounting his life story but writing about the subject he knew best: Shakespeare. This final chapter was markedly different in tone and content from the rest of the book. It drew upon Burton's skills in interpreting Shakespeare, showing Burton the scholar, the role that the former pupil most admired. This won Richard Burton's approval.

Philip Burton's success in the moulding of the young actor's innate talent was tested in various ways. The YMCA provided one venue for this. In *Youth at the Helm* Richard played an American businessman. He also gained some vital experience in BBC broadcasting in Cardiff in Burton's radio dramatisation of Francis Brett Young's Mercian novel *The House Under the Water*, published in 1932. Long before *The Last Days of Dolwyn* (Emlyn Williams' account of the flooding of a Welsh village to supply water to Liverpudlians which became Richard's first film in 1949), Burton's radio play provided a semi-fictionalised account of the building of the Elan Valley Reservoirs at the turn of the

century. These reservoirs were constructed to provide water for the people of Birmingham. Burton added at the last moment an extra scene specially written for Richard.[138]

And ironically, Richard played the part of Professor Higgins in the Sec's production of *Pygmalion*. In October 1943 Bernard Shaw's play ran for a week at the YMCA. The *Port Talbot Guardian* praised the casting and noted that Richard Jenkins 'displayed dramatic talent that made him a dominating personality, and brought out all that was best in the acting of his opposite number, Dilys Jones'.[139] By now Richard had passed his school certificate, doing best in English literature and mathematics, two subjects that Burton had taught at the Sec. His life was about to change rapidly and irrevocably.

In the month after *Pygmalion,* Richard made his debut as a professional actor in the Royal Court, Liverpool. Philip Burton had responded to Emlyn Williams' appeal for Welsh actors in his new play *The Druid's Rest*, Richard had impressed at his audition at the Sandringham Hotel in Cardiff. After 'a dismal procession of "No Goods"' there appeared 'a boy of seventeen, of startling beauty, and quiet intelligence'. He had looked, Williams declared more than forty years later, 'imperishable'.[140] And the first step was taken in Richard Burton's professional career. Yet after all that perfecting of English accents, it was a voice with Welsh cadences that was required for the play.[141] When *The Druid's Rest* came to Cardiff, the young actor's proud family saw him on stage. It opened in London in January 1944.

Richard Jenkins had turned eighteen on 10 November 1943. He left school at the end of term. In a delicious understatement, the school magazine wished Richie Jenkins 'as much success and popularity in his stage career as he won in Leisan House, for we know that this will ensure his success'.[142] Just before Christmas, he became Burton's ward (the age difference between him and Burton was twenty days short of the minimum age difference of twenty-one years so he could not be formally adopted).[143]

Philip Burton remained his guardian until Richard was twenty-one. Thanks to his ATC training, in the spring of 1944 Richard spent six months at Oxford University (Exeter College) attached to the Royal Air Force. Over time there would be a radical shift in the power relations that had existed between the two men: this was not an easy transition but it was inevitable as the former pupil metamorphosed into Richard Burton, one of the most famous figures in the world.

Although he would return to Port Talbot and in increasing style, Richard had effectively left behind the town that had made him. At the end of the war Philip Burton also moved on. His final production at the Sec was *The Lady with a Lamp* in 1945. He left in July and his fellow schoolmaster Horace James wrote in the *Wayfarer* about Burton's remarkable ability to inspire his pupils in literature classes. As for the school plays, such was his skill that 'each heroine, in turn, felt herself an Edith Evans, and each hero, a Gielgud'.[144]

Burton became a features producer for the BBC in Cardiff before moving to London. He adapted for the radio Rhys Davies' novel *Marianne* (partly set in a steel town called Port Trolon[145]). In 1954 he went to the United States, where he enjoyed an illustrious career in his own right and he stayed there for the rest of his life. He remained close to Richard and clearly identified with him as family. In 1957 Richard stayed with him. When he was about to be joined by Sybil and their baby Kate, Philip Burton commented, 'It will be pleasant to have all the Burtons together for a season.'[146] *The Dark Wood*, the last of the many plays he wrote, was set in south Wales and intended for Richard. Philip Burton later explained that the actor had 'wanted to do it, but death intervened'.[147]

Richard Burton had died in Switzerland in August 1984. But he has not disappeared from this book and his relationship with the town in his years of fame will be explored in later chapters. As for the erstwhile Senior Master at Port Talbot Secondary

School, he outlived his former pupil and protégé, dying in 1995 in his ninety-first year. Philip Burton had spent his last months in an Episcopalian nursing home in Florida but his ashes were buried in his parents' grave at Mountain Ash. The impact he had made on numerous pupils and other aspirant actors from Port Talbot was a lasting one and the tradition that Burton, Meredith Jones and Leo Lloyd established of mentoring and enabling promising youngsters to flourish would be replicated by others in the town, as we shall see in the following chapters.

2

Enter Anthony Hopkins

On New Year's Eve in 1937, the year that Richard Jenkins began at the Sec, another international star was born in Port Talbot. Anthony Hopkins' birthplace was a modern, semi-detached house in Wern Road, Margam. Although he experienced the war as a small child, his upbringing was, in a number of respects, privileged compared to that of many in his locality. He was an only child and the family business was prospering. Dick Hopkins had inherited his father's bakery in town, in Tanygroes Street. Richard Hopkins Senior, a master baker and confectioner from nearby Neath, had learned the confectionary side of his trade for Peek Frean in Bermondsey where their early adoption of a nine-hour day would have appealed to this dedicated socialist.

Philip Anthony Hopkins attended Groes Primary School (as would I some years later). It was originally a Victorian Church of England School supported financially by the heiress Emily Talbot, who rewarded children's regular attendance with a penny a week. She hosted an annual tea party in the servants' hall at Margam Castle where pupils were presented with lengths of cloth to be made into dresses and suits. It was taken over by the local authority in 1903 and the M4 would, in time, obliterate both school and village.

Despite having friends and his cousin Bobby Hayes living close by, Anthony was a quiet and somewhat self-sufficient child. He devoured information from encyclopaedias. Just as Cis

49

James had doted on her little brother Richard Jenkins, so Anthony's mother Muriel adored him. Once the war ended he accompanied his grandparents on holidays to a small farm in the village of Willersey in the Cotswolds (years later he genuflected to his fond memories of this time in a musical composition entitled *Evesham Fair*).

In 1947 the family moved to live above the business. The trade of Jones the Baker was, like the town, expanding and before long he acquired larger premises on Taibach's main thoroughfare, Commercial Road. Here – within a stone's throw of where Richard Jenkins had worked in drapery – was the thriving bakery, a bread shop and the family home.

For a time Anthony attended the Central Boys' School but concerned at his lack of interest and educational progress in state schools to date, his parents opted for private education. In the autumn of 1949 he started as one of a small number of boarders at West Monmouth School many miles away in Pontypool. It was not a success, and after five terms he was enrolled nearer to home at Cowbridge Grammar School with its proud tradition of learning. This dated back to the early seventeenth century when the benefactor, Sir Leoline Jenkins of Jesus College, Oxford had endowed the school.

By the time Anthony was a pupil it had both fee-paying and direct-grant pupils. Its head teacher's main (but not to be underestimated) distinction was that he had played rugby for Wales. It retained a belief in the virtues of a classical education. Being neither sporty nor academically minded, Anthony was miserable. Once again he was in a minority as a boarder and it was a draconian regime. He did, however, learn to be an effective mimic of his teachers.[148] The Port Talbot actor Norman Comer knew Anthony Hopkins in London and remembers him as a marvellous mimic with a brilliant impersonation of Jack Hawkins in *The Cruel Sea*.

Anthony spent four unhappy years at the school, seeking

refuge in playing the piano. Here was an activity that did not involve a team effort. He quickly abandoned piano tuition at school but not his love of playing. Patrick Hannan, who was a fellow pupil, later wrote that Anthony 'spent much of his time slumped over the battered upright piano in the schoolroom, playing music of shattering melancholy'.[149] Back home, to the bemusement of his father, he would entertain himself by playing Beethoven on the piano his mother had bought him for £5. Aged twelve he began composing melodies. He impressed Iris Thomas, his piano teacher in Baglan.

The plan for private schooling had misfired. Anthony emerged with O level English and little else beyond insecurity, a belief that he was not an achiever, and a disdain for formal education. It was not a situation that his father, a congenital worrier, found easy to accept. Anthony sought refuge again in playing the piano and in going to the pictures on Friday nights. Like Richard Jenkins, he too frequented the nearby Regent Cinema and the Picturedrome where he managed to get in free sometimes: his friend Brian's grandfather owned it.

There were now also some salubrious, even luxurious, cinemas to choose from in Port Talbot, the newest being the Odeon and the Plaza. The Odeon in the centre of town (originally the Majestic) boasted central heating and spacious plush seating. The Plaza was handy, seated 1,600 and its art-deco design appealing. Wartime building restrictions had meant that although it showed its first film in April 1940 (*Babes in Arms*, starring Mickey Rooney and Judy Garland), features such as its distinctive cream tiles and Plaza sign were only installed in the early fifties.[150] Here Anthony watched Humphrey Bogart in *Sahara* and was mesmerised.

Port Talbot was thriving in the 1950s when Anthony was a teenager. This also meant that the landscape of his childhood was changing dramatically. The Works had gradually increased production from the 1930s and by the time war broke out were

at full capacity.[151] Post-war production moved away from heavy steel products to strip steel production. The new Steel Company of Wales oversaw the construction of a vast hot-strip mill on Margam Moors, employing more than 7,000 men housed at an old RAF base at nearby Stormy Down.

Opened in 1951, it was one of Britain's largest industrial projects. The Abbey Works boasted the leading strip mill in Britain and Europe. Tinplate and sheet production were stimulated by increased consumer demand, especially for motorcars. Increased profits followed. The Steel Company of Wales became Wales' largest single employer and by the 1960s was exporting to seventy-five countries. This steelworks led the way in terms of output and witnessed a huge increase in numbers working in the nationalised industry between 1951 and 1960. In that year employment peaked at 18,352.[152]

Work could also be found at the docks that received the iron ore and in the British Oxygen Company built in 1951 to supply oxygen and nitrogen, chiefly to the steelworks. The town was booming, with a population approaching 52,000 by the early 1960s. Wages were high. Thursdays meant payday in what was now known as 'Treasure Island'. Pubs and workingmen's clubs were buzzing.

One of the town's most energetic advocates was the entertainer Bryn Thomas. In the mid-fifties 'Uncle Bryn', as he was known, was producing pantomimes with Marlene Evans at the YMCA. Five-week runs were sell-outs.[153] By the sixties this ex-Olympic hockey player and rugby coach was the sports officer at the new sports and leisure seaside complex the Afan Lido (run by Richard Burton's younger brother). By night Thomas ran, in the heart of old Aberafan, a mini-casino called the Carlton Club, where the rich and famous – including rugby stars and even Elizabeth Taylor – could be seen as well as us locals. The Carlton featured in the evocative litany of Port Talbot's lost history at the end of *The Passion* in 2011.

The desire for even better times saw the enactment of Port Talbot's own version of a bad 'B' movie. The greedy John Rivers, mistakenly believing that the payroll for the steelworks was held in the vaults of the Midland Bank in Station Road, had the idea of renting an empty shop opposite and tunnelling under the main road in order to rob the bank. He recruited two brothers to do the hard work. But Rivers had failed to pay the shop rent on time. The landlord called in to collect it and found the place covered in earth – the brothers had already shifted ten tons of it – so the police paid them a visit. Rivers was never apprehended.[154]

Anthony's life lacked the purpose not only of the town's villains but also of those with a career plan. Unsure what to do and lacking formal qualifications, he took several casual jobs. He was employed briefly in the Works as a stores assistant. He also tried baking bread. Neither job appealed. But on 18 February 1955, when he was seventeen, something happened that had a profound impact on the direction his life would take. Encouraged by his father to get out and do something, Anthony, his cousin and a friend went to play snooker at the nearby YMCA where Richard Jenkins had performed. That evening he met a man called Cyril Jenkins, the producer for the YMCA Players. As a result of this the young man would gain the opportunity to realise his talent.

On 1 January 1973, the world-famous actor Anthony Hopkins wrote a letter to Cyril Jenkins. He recalled how Jenkins had given him his first part, adding, 'If you hadn't I probably would never have gone into the Theatre profession'.[155] He had heard that Jenkins was ill. Just two days later Cyril Jenkins died aged sixty-nine.

So who was this man who made such an impact? If Richard Jenkins had Leo Lloyd and Philip Burton to inspire and train him, then the railwayman producer Cyril Jenkins, Port Talbot born and bred, was Anthony Hopkins' equivalent.

The YMCA Players' successor to Burton had been Peter

Gyngell, RADA trained and, in the words of Doug Rees (the Players' secretary at the time and later president of the National Union of Journalists), 'an outstanding, ebullient character'. Gyngell put on four productions a year but then emigrated. Jenkins was invited to take over. At the AGM in February 1955, Gyngell stated that if they followed Cyril Jenkins they would have 'the finest dramatic society in South Wales', adding 'and you deserve it'.[156]

Born in 1903 into a coal mining family in the Velindre area of town (the same district as Anthony Hopkins' beloved grandfather Fred Yeats), Jenkins was the youngest of seven children. By the age of fourteen he had left Aberavon National Schools and was earning his living. His sister Ruth Lavinia was a performer: she and her husband Harry Walmer ran a pierrot troupe that toured seaside towns. Young Jenkins also developed a taste for entertaining and became a boy soprano in variety shows, even singing on the London stage. After his voice broke, however, he took a secure job as a porter for the Great Western Railway (GWR).

Jenkins spent his entire working life on the railways. He was a goods clerk in the inter-war years and later a supervisory foreman, eventually retiring in 1968. But he was equally busy outside his paid employment. He dedicated himself to the theatre both as an actor and as a producer.[157] He once admitted, 'I have always had this bug but my wife really developed it in me'. He had married the equally remarkable Clarice Rees in 1928. The daughter of an engine driver, she had gone to the Sec then to secretarial college in Cardiff. She became a renowned elocutionist[158] and was a triple National Eisteddfod winner as well as scooping a vast number of other prizes.

Over the next decade the couple gained considerable experience in local theatricals. For the Zion Dramatic Society, 'Madame Clarice Rees-Jenkins, Port Talbot, an elocutionist of national fame, and her husband, Mr Cyril Jenkins' produced

and had the lead roles in *The Optimist*, a three-act comedy at the New Hall, complete with Madame Short's orchestra. Cyril Jenkins was the producer (at the same venue) for a number of modern plays for the Taibach and Port Talbot Co-operative Amateur Dramatic Society, including Clemence Dane's controversial drama *A Bill of Divorcement*.

Although the Port Talbot Little Theatre is usually credited as starting rather later, by August 1938 Jenkins and his actors had parted company with the Co-operative Drama Society and met together to form 'the nucleus of a Little Theatre' and so give Drama in Port Talbot 'a progressive lift.'[159] By early November it had fifty-one members. It planned to debate and offer advice to playwrights and invited those interested in any form of Drama to enrol. It was explained that they had been formed for an educational purpose and that lectures would be given in dramatic art, make-up and production. Rehearsals were underway for their first production, *Hamlet*, to be produced by Jenkins.[160] War, however, put paid to the theatre's plans for the time being.

War also halted temporarily the GWR Festival at Reading, an event at which Jenkins enjoyed outstanding success. This annual festival of Music and Drama had been started in 1923, organised by the general secretary of the GWR Social and Educational Union. Reading's large and small town halls and a church were commandeered for the occasions. By 1938 there were 3,000 competitors from Cornwall to Essex and the event lasted five days. Welsh entrants included the Hirwaun Western Players, whilst speech and music competitors came from places such as Barry, Swansea, Pembrey and Llanelli. In 1936 the Hugh Mytton Cup for performing a scene from Shakespeare – *Hamlet* in this instance – was won by Port Talbot, bringing it to Wales for the first time (London and Swindon had previously monopolised it). Jenkins and the Port Talbot Shakespearean Society won the cup for three years in succession.

In 1938, as tension mounted in Europe, Guy Pertwee the

adjudicator declared that Jenkins in the Trial scene from *The Merchant of Venice* provided 'one of the best performances of Shylock I have ever seen'. The Port Talbot acting team included Clarice Jenkins as Portia (she also sang in women's choirs at the event), her sister Betty Rees, four goods clerks and an engine cleaner. The couple now had a two-year-old daughter, Marilyn, who was the youngest competitor at Reading, an elf in the children's musical play *The Wishing Well* directed by her father (and for which he earned one of the four medals he won that year).

Their triumphs were reported annually in the national press. In 1937, when Port Talbot's *Othello* took the cup, the *Daily Express* explained in somewhat patronising tones that: 'Every day to you and me, the husbands are just railway porters, firemen, signalmen, or shunters, but to-day they are Romeos, kings, knights and courtiers.' In that same year Jenkins and the Port Talbot group performed a one-act play called *In the Tunnel*. Perhaps it took realism too far – all eight characters die from suffocation – as it only took third prize.

By 1948 the Festival had resumed and Jenkins, who had worked in Swansea during the war, was back producing plays there and in his hometown. He even put on a two-act Children's Operetta for the Port Talbot branch of the British Railways Staff Association in which Marilyn was a princess.[161] He produced for the new Globe Players and was chosen by the committee organising the town's celebrations of the Festival of Britain to produce the theatrical contribution to 1951. It was a selection from *The Merchant of Venice* in which Evan Morgan (who had been taught by Philip Burton) was Shylock and Hubert Davies was Salanio.

Drama Clubs at the Central School were organised and taught by Clarice Jenkins. Pupils did choral speaking as well as performing in plays. She enhanced her reputation by coaching (from home) pupils for Guildhall examinations in Speech and Drama.

Meanwhile Cyril Jenkins took on an additional role as assistant Warden and Drama Tutor at Trefelin[162] County Youth Centre at Trefelin County Secondary School, sponsored by Glamorgan County Council and run on the same lines as the Taibach Centre that Richard Jenkins had attended.

These youth centres or clubs participated in Youth Drama Festivals. Here Leo Lloyd and Cyril Jenkins, the town's outstanding theatrical exponents for young people, were in competition with each other. All the youth clubs of the town would come together in an annual festival run by the Port Talbot and Glyncorrwg Youth Service Association. There were numerous other competitions and Youth Drama Festivals throughout the year. In 1953, for example, Lloyd and Jenkins' productions were tied first at Aberdare with eighty marks apiece. Lloyd (Taibach) was praised for being a 'great technician' and Jenkins (Trefelin) for 'the born artistry' of his production (of J. M. Synge's *Riders to the Sea*).[163]

So when Anthony Hopkins met Cyril Jenkins that evening the raw recruit was encountering the YMCA's new producer, but one who was already very experienced, an acknowledged 'magnificent exponent of Shakespeare' and also used to working with lads from non-theatrical backgrounds. Doug Rees has stressed how fortunate the small group of YMCA Players were with their producers: 'They instilled a belief that we could tackle anything.'

There are several accounts of Anthony's conversion narrative in circulation but it seems that he expressed an interest in seeing the group's rehearsals so was taken to watch Jenkins coach young Elved Lody in an extract from *Othello* for a forthcoming Drama Festival. Anthony was 'hooked'. He had found something that fascinated him and admits that 'I suddenly felt at home for the first time in my life'.[164] Jenkins worked with him, building up his confidence and voice. Those who witnessed the transformation have commented on how this withdrawn boy threw himself into rehearsals.

Part of Jenkins' new plan for the Players was to do an Easter Play. This is not to be confused with *Emmanuel*, usually credited as Anthony Hopkins' first role. The latter was put on in December. First came *The Easter Story*. Jean Edgar (later Lody) was 'A young and promising' Mary Magdalen and remembers Anthony as a somewhat clumsy centurion guarding the tomb of Jesus. It was here that he delivered the well-known and somewhat prescient single line: 'Blessed are the meek for they shall inherit the earth.'

Pat Dorman was one of the girls doing Drama in the evenings at the Trefelin Centre and later trained to be a drama teacher. She remembers acting with Anthony in the final act of *Othello* on one of the many occasions that Jenkins prepared these young people to perform scenes from Shakespeare in drama competitions. According to Doug Rees, Jenkins maintained that 'if you can understand the Drama in what Shakespeare wrote, you can do anything'. The young woman was worried about how to die as Desdemona but she also recalls rehearsing with:

> ... a new and shy boy of my age who was called Tony. He had just left school and joined our group but was very quiet and hardly able to speak but when he did had a lovely rich, slow and hesitant voice which held us in a slight anxiety about whether he would actually manage to get his words out. Cyril was kind to him and unusually patient so we once again won the competition... but even though Anthony Hopkins only had a line to say I think he stole the show.

She remembers him playing the piano at the Taibach home of her friend Joan Cullen. All three were involved in choral speaking for an Eisteddfod (probably the county youth Eisteddfod held in Porthcawl in 1955). Anthony had a solo in this and they won again. They used to practise their speeches at the Jenkins' home in Station Road. Some years later Anthony

signed a photograph for Cyril. It says 'With many, many fond memories & thanks – for all the cups of tea and bowls of soup and help in setting me on the way'. Refreshments followed rehearsals.

The YMCA's winter programme was showcased in late September 1955 with a number of different events. They included a one-act play called *Michael*, adapted by Miles Malleson from a translation of Tolstoy's story 'What Men Live By'. Some of Anthony's fellow actors remember him in this play. He was playing the part of the Angel Michael who is exiled from heaven and discovered in the snow by a peasant family who take him in, seeing him simply as a youth who needs help. He has disobeyed God's command and as part of his penance has to learn three lessons. He comes to understand 'what men live by' through witnessing how the family take him in and share what little they have with him.

This was Anthony's first challenging role. The play was about thirty minutes long. Michael does not speak until he has learned the third lesson. In a lengthy speech he then has to reveal his true identity and what he has been taught. The need both to convey his actions and emotions in silence and then to deliver the all-important final speech required serious application and was especially exacting for young newcomers. The script used by the actors included a note explaining that the part of Michael:

> demands a player who can act simply and who has an instinctive sense of poetry. If his long final speech has the least tone of insincerity or sanctimoniousness or theatrical straining after effect, it will be ruined.[165]

It added that amateur actors required 'sincerity and enthusiasm and hard work' to perform this play effectively.

Fred Steadman-Jones (Cyril Jenkins' son-in-law), a former member of the YMCA Players at this time and later a university

drama lecturer, suggests that this would probably have been 'the finest experience that this introverted young man could have worked on at that point in his life'. He also believes that Cyril Jenkins' greatest gift to the young actor was his emphasis on the importance of studying a script intently in advance, something he demonstrated in part by example. Jenkins always carried with him a copy of whatever play he was producing and would even study it during breaks at work. Anthony Hopkins is known for learning his scripts thoroughly before rehearsals begin, as well as studying carefully the levels of meaning in them.

Anthony also helped out with stage management. In September the Players took Sutton Vane's play *Outward Bound* (which was first produced in London in 1923 and turned into a film in 1930) to the Rhayader Drama Festival in mid-Wales. Set on a modern liner, it explored the consequences of human behaviour: its passengers are no longer alive and each one is sailing towards a final destiny of heaven or hell. The YMCA Players didn't win but the production was praised. Three weeks later they opened the new season at home with this play. The *Gazette* was very enthusiastic about the production and noted that 'Stage management was safe in the hands of Anthony Hopkins and Duncan Miles' (who chaired the society).[166]

Then came the December 1955 production of James Forsyth's *Emmanuel* in which Anthony was famously cast as Justinius, a Roman Procurator.[167] Jenkins produced it and had a modest role as a shepherd. The *Port Talbot Guardian* was a little critical of the production because its sixteen scenes demanded nifty work backstage. The critic also felt that the season's programme might have produced plays 'in a lighter vein'.[168] In what has proved to be something of an under-estimation, the *Glamorgan Gazette* described the YMCA Players as a young group 'with some talented performers who will undoubtedly make their mark on local dramatics in the years ahead'.[169]

So motivated had Anthony become that he had applied for a two-year scholarship (worth £100 a year) to study at the Welsh College of Music and Drama at Cardiff. He had spotted the advertisement for the Prince Littler[170] scholarship in the *Western Mail*. Dr Raymond Edwards (later the college's long-serving principal) was running the drama department in a college that had been initially dedicated to music. The gifted son of a north Walian miner, it was he who built up, with his wife June Griffiths and others, the fledgling drama department housed in the grounds of Cardiff Castle from 1951.

Anthony was interviewed in Cardiff City Hall. His choice for the ten-minute audition was, appropriately enough, a scene from *Othello* (as it would later be for his audition with Olivier, who was already playing that part). Anthony was accepted by Edwards, who was prepared to take a gamble on this young man with little in the way of academic qualifications and but a short acquaintance with the stage. Edwards' intuition told him that the teenager had an energy and voice that would go far. He believed that south Walian actors had an inbred propensity to project their voices due to generations of miners having worked in conditions with foul air and cramped conditions. The lack of oxygen meant that they had acquired a habit of breathing deeply into their lungs, dilating their nostrils and stretching and opening their air passages. He recognised that this was 'something Hopkins had, before I taught him anything'.[171] Moreover 'he moved with a very animal energy' and he also had 'the voice of Burton'.

Whilst he was a drama student, Anthony made his television debut in a non-speaking role (for which he earned threepence) as one of the pupils at the little school run by Miss Moffat in Emlyn Williams' classic *The Corn is Green*. It was a live recording on a Sunday evening in January 1956 from the BBC's Lime Grove studios in London. Flora Robson (who played Miss Moffat) had chosen him at an audition in Cardiff.

The two years at Cardiff were followed by a post as an assistant stage manager and some acting in a sixteen-week Arts Council tour of *Look Back in Anger* and *She Stoops to Conquer*, then a much less stimulating stint doing National Service which consisted of office work in a military training camp in the south of England. Demobbed in 1960, Anthony became part of a short-lived but significant experiment in professional touring theatre for Welsh actors, championed by the patron of Welsh arts, Richard Rhys (the 9th Baron of Dynevor from 1962). Thomas Taig, a distinguished academic and a founder of Swansea's Little Theatre, was now lecturing at the Welsh College of Drama. Anthony was chosen for the lead in a drama for Rhys' Merlin Theatre Group. Directed by Taig, *Have a Cigarette* was the English version of a Saunders Lewis play. Set in East Berlin and based on fact, it tells of a young communist charged with assassinating a diplomat and his last-moment conversion to Christianity.

The play toured south Wales. Anthony's mother saw it in Swansea but it also came to Port Talbot where it was put on at the Great Hall at Sandfields Comprehensive. The schoolboy Norman Comer watched it. A few years later Comer went to RADA. Anthony Hopkins was a year ahead of him (Hopkins started there in 1961). Comer remembers how he cringed when he asked him about the play. Hopkins has acknowledged elsewhere that he had been lacking in experience and that his real hero at the time was James Dean: 'So I thought acting was just about looking miserable and scuffling around'.[172] But he had returned to Port Talbot as a professional actor and would, before long, embark on a spectacular career.

Anthony Hopkins had not flourished when young but he had found a supportive institution and mentor rather closer to home than his school. As it happened he was fortunate that it was the YMCA that caught his teenage imagination but it could have been one of the other local organisations that promoted the stage. An acting tradition was already sufficiently developed in

the town to continue to inspire its youth.

Support for acting was even shown by local industrialists. The steel company Richard Thomas & Baldwins Ltd encouraged drama groups, sent two of its most promising amateur students (Connie Longman and Beryl Stephens) to do a course at the British Drama League in London[173] and engaged Richard Blythe, a lecturer and coach who had been in the Donald Wolfit Company, to run a class in poetry, prose and play-reading at their Byass and Wern Works. Company members performed plays that Blythe produced. Clive Jenkins, later General Secretary of the Association of Scientific Technical and Managerial Staff, played a politician in 1945 in their production of *Twentieth Century Lullaby*.[174] In the mid-fifties Leo Lloyd produced winning plays in the Steel Company of Wales' annual inter-departmental Drama Festival.

The grammar schools still did their bit, both the County School Players and the Wayfarers (as the former Sec pupils called themselves from 1951). They included Dennis Burgess, Cliff Jones, Brinley Jenkins and Dilys Jones, who had all been trained by Philip Burton. Four years later they were just beaten into second place by Brecon in the Welsh area finals of the British Drama League's Festival of one-act plays at Aberdare.[175] At the school Philip Burton was hardly an easy act to follow. But he had a worthy successor in Selwyn Davies. As Davies admitted, long before he joined the staff: 'Everywhere I turned, the spectre of P. H. Burton haunted one... he had, indeed, managed to attain a rare distinction by becoming a legend during his own lifetime'.[176]

Davies taught English, embraced contemporary poetry and put on the school play. It had become an integral and cherished part of the calendar. Davies wrote plays for his pupils, ensuring that there were good parts for girls as well as boys and reworked some well-known dramas. The first was *Nell Gwynne*. As a reviewer noted, it played down the 'love interest', emphasising other aspects of Nell Gwynne's life such as her efforts to help

soldiers injured in battle.[177]

The actress Francine Morgan has explained how her mother had come under the spell of Selwyn Davies at Dyffryn Grammar School (as the Sec was called from 1953). He 'really gave them all a love of literature... I had *Macbeth* quoted to me before I could walk, I reckon'. Another of Davies's pupils at Dyffryn was Godfrey Evans. He has noted how the school encouraged a 'can do' attitude that enabled many to flourish. Evans would in turn become a pivotal figure in the development of many an actor. He would inspire the young Michael Sheen.

Like Richard Burton before them, both Anthony Hopkins and Michael Sheen found encouragement for their talents through individuals from Port Talbot who managed to give them discipline and yet the freedom to be imaginative. At the same time they learned to become part a team of actors as well as developing an appetite for being focused.

3

Michael Sheen's Time

Unlike Richard Burton and Anthony Hopkins, Michael Sheen was not born in the Port Talbot area. Yet given how strongly he identifies with the place – despite being based in Los Angeles – it is easy to presume that he is a native of the town. He was born on 5 February 1969 in the steel town of Newport, Monmouthshire.[178] His father was a personnel manager. The family lived in the village of Llanmartin but moved to Merseyside when Michael was five. His ability to integrate himself into his surroundings was immediately apparent as he adopted a Liverpudlian accent. His mother recalls him going to school at St George's Primary School in Wallasey: 'He started on the Tuesday. By the Friday I couldn't understand a word he was saying.' At the end of his first term he was performing on the school stage.

Port Talbot was the hometown of Michael's parents Meyrick and Irene and three years later they moved back there. Michael and his younger sister Joanne grew up in Baglan. Nearby at Baglan Bay was one of the largest petro-chemical works in Europe. But from Baglan you could look down on the sea, and it was not far to the long sandy beach at Aberafan and its Miami Beach funfair invoking the earlier American-inspired Coney Beach in Porthcawl.

After Blaenbaglan Primary School, Michael attended Glan Afan Comprehensive,[179] the former County School. A clever child, Michael was especially good at English and Drama but

his real love as a young teenager was football. He had supported Liverpool when he was living on the Wirral and being skilled at the game now helped to integrate him as an outsider into the local community. At the age of just eight, he was playing for Baglan Boys under-12s.

Richard Jenkins might have dreamed of rugby honours, but Michael Sheen came close to training as a professional footballer. As a twelve-year-old he was talent spotted as a possible for Arsenal's Youth Team.[180] He was on holiday with his parents at Pontins on the Isle of Wight. The young Tony Adams, already playing for the team, was there too. His father Alex Adams noted Michael's footballing skills and talked to Michael's parents, as did the club. But the Sheens were wary, convinced that their son was too young to be in London on his own, even though Arsenal would have taken responsibility for him and his education. They were not keen to move again. Adams secured a couple of trials for the young Michael with Welsh teams but this was soon overtaken by other events.

Michael also enjoyed music from a young age. He was a schoolboy at a time when state support for the subject in various forms was encouraged. He discovered a talent for playing the trumpet (fellow Welsh actor Ioan Gruffudd was a good oboist in his youth). Michael took lessons and got the opportunity to perform with the West Glamorgan Youth Band. But practice sessions clashed with football. Soon, however, both passions gave way to acting. Michael Sheen has, nevertheless, suggested that football and acting share a number of characteristics. He sees both as part of a team effort in which sharing is vital. 'Players pass the ball to each other like actors handling the text, and acting is also about scoring goals, getting through to the end of an act.' The theatre and the football pitch are both sites of pleasure and expectation and both, he has argued, can produce 'grace under pressure'.[181] Years later he played the football manager Brian Clough in *The Damned United*.

The key to Michael's commitment to the stage lay in West Glamorgan Youth Theatre Company (WGYTC). In 1974 local government reorganisation saw Port Talbot become part of West Glamorgan. An ambitious, well-structured plan for drama followed, culminating in the formation of the youth theatre. Behind this were far-sighted educational policy makers[182] and Godfrey Evans.

He had been born further east in Aberfan in 1941 but his father obtained work in Port Talbot's dry dock when Godfrey was tiny, so the family moved. Although not from a theatrical or teaching background he had a model theatre as a child. A favourite aunt who was a primary school head teacher in Herefordshire and with whom he would spend his summer holidays was also an influence. He was fortunate enough to be taught by Selwyn Davies at Dyffryn and had a small part in Davies's *Nell Gwynne* when he was fourteen. The following year he secured the lead role as Becket in *Murder in the Cathedral*.

Evans regularly attended Bridge Street Baptist Chapel with his family. Here he learned to recite verse. Leo Lloyd's wife Maggie was a member of the chapel and Leo Lloyd, who attended occasionally, spotted the youngster. He offered twelve-year-old Godfrey the part of the page in the Jean Anouilh version of *Antigone* being put on at the Drama Club. He had just six lines to speak but relished the opportunity. Lloyd's production would win at least five first prizes at Welsh Drama Festivals.

Lloyd had formed this Port Talbot Drama Club after the disbanding of his Thespian Players in the war. In 1943, the Drama Club's production of *The Barretts of Wimpole Street* had won first prize in the competition held in Pontycymmer (Bristol came second) and the Bath adjudicator declared that many of the scenes 'reached almost "greatness"'.[183] Lloyd was a frequent lecturer at summer schools run by the Glamorgan Education Committee and a familiar face at the Urdd.[184] In 1956, aged 65, he was awarded the MBE for his services to

Amateur Drama in Glamorgan's youth movement, the first person in Wales to receive civil honours for such work. At a dinner in Port Talbot, at which he was presented with a gold watch, he spoke eloquently of the virtues of drama, arguing that 'It keeps us stable in this topsy turvey world'.[185] He added that the fine young people he had trained were 'all over the world and, I am pleased to say, are still participating in drama, either producing or acting, or both'.

After *Antigone* Lloyd (who had already helped to develop Richard Jenkins' acting skills) suggested that Evans become part of his group at Taibach Youth Centre. Although not officially old enough (membership was for fourteen- to twenty-five-year-olds) he let him join. Evans remembers Lloyd as an instinctive director passionately involved with his plays. So respected were his players that in 1956 they were invited to take part in the All-Wales Drama Festival held in Newtown, Montgomeryshire by the Drama Council of Wales. It was the first time that a youth session had been included.

Some of these Taibach actors were young men who had done national service. They would work on Shakespeare several nights a week then get put through their paces in Lloyd's home. 'It was agony,' recalls Evans 'because he was so precise and such a perfectionist.' They practiced until they got their scene right, then 'the next week he'd tear you to bits again'. Many a time Evans went home in tears. But he kept going back. Fortunately for the youngsters of Port Talbot, Evans also returned to the town after training as a drama teacher at Central.

Aberavon's MP since 1929 had been the socialist W. G. Cove. As president of the National Association of Labour Teachers he had been an outspoken advocate of comprehensive education in the post-war Labour government. In 1958, the year before he retired and before the Labour government granted local education authorities a mandate to plan for comprehensive

education, Port Talbot had pioneered the first purpose-built comprehensive school in Wales at Sandfields. It included a Great Hall capable of accommodating an audience of up to 1,200.

Year after year I used to watch the local operatic society perform their annual operettas there. Before long the school would have 2,000 pupils. These were heady days. Teachers were young, highly committed and enjoyed the opportunity to be involved from the start in such an innovative atmosphere. As one of the first Sandfields teachers explained: 'People used to come in droves from across the UK to see the state of the art facilities'.[186] Godfrey Evans was appointed in 1963 as the drama specialist within the school's English department. Over eleven years he built up a strong and separate drama department. He recalls the joy of operating in such an atmosphere and how invigorating it was for those in the performing arts to work with pupils where 'you don't have to cut through the flannel'. He relished their openness and directness. In a community composed of incomers from near and far for work in the steel industry, there was what he has called 'a healthy transference of cultures' and a sense of being outward-looking. He took pupils to Cardiff and Stratford to see productions.

They, in turn, valued what Evans and the school offered. One actor inspired by him was Philip Joseph who played the part of George Harrison in Willy Russell's smash hit *John, Paul, George, Ringo and Bert*, which premiered at the Liverpool Everyman in 1974 with a stellar cast before transferring to London's Lyric Theatre for a year.

Francine Morgan, Gareth Snook and Derek Hutchinson are other talented actors who were amongst Godfrey Evans' early pupils at Sandfields. Morgan was able to study four languages (the curriculum included Russian) and was taught Italian O level in the lunch and assembly breaks by her French teacher. Not long after leaving drama school Morgan secured an Italian-

speaking part in *The Aspern Papers* at Guildford and London's Haymarket Theatre with Wendy Hiller and Vanessa Redgrave.

All Sandfields pupils had one weekly drama lesson in their first three years and the option to take drama exams after that. Evans' pupils were amongst the first in the UK to do Drama at CSE level. He embedded it into the heart of the school.[187] For Morgan the department exuded 'an air of something extraordinary'. She recalls seeing plays such as *Mother Courage* there and a *Hamlet* in the round: 'It made many of us long to be part of it.' She soon was.

From this base, and building upon the fact that the old Glamorgan Education Authority had prided itself on strong advisory services across the curriculum (especially in music), Evans was also appointed Drama Adviser for the new authority. Drama centres were set up to which recommended students had free weekly access and where teachers from schools and advisory teachers developed their skills after school. Port Talbot pupils went to the centre at Cwrt Sart Comprehensive School in Briton Ferry. Drama classes in primary schools were also developed at this time and residential courses were created for both primary and secondary pupils.

At the top of this pyramid stood the new WGYTC. Many aspired to join it. Competition was tough, with auditions held in schools for those already identified as promising and nominated by teachers. Godfrey Evans was appointed its Director in 1975. In his first year he spent a week in schools auditioning between eighty and 100 hopefuls – already identified by their teachers – in all the West Glamorgan Schools. Forty-one were chosen, including about ten production and technical students. West Glamorgan students would put on a summer play and another one at Christmas. At Dan-y-Coed, their residential centre in Swansea, mid-weekly rehearsals and three residential weekends took place, as well as blocks of rehearsals as each show approached. At the same time there

would be studio classes in movement, improvised drama and voice and speech, so that there was always something in which to be involved.

The first production was *The Winter's Tale*. It was performed in the drama hall at Dyffryn School. Students became used to many different kinds of stages. This was part of a decision not to work simply from the conventional proscenium stage but to experience a variety of venues, from schools to Taliesin Theatre at Swansea University, the Sherman Theatre in Cardiff, arts centres and even inside Margam Orangery and outside in Margam Park.

So by the time Michael Sheen became interested in acting there had been established a solid basis for students to develop drama beyond school. Yet he almost missed his chance to study it at Glan Afan since he initially opted to study French instead. Fortunately this was one subject that he didn't excel in and he changed subjects, much to the relief of the drama teacher Ken Tucker, who recognised from the start that there was something about this student's appetite for developing himself. Michael was soon willing to participate in anything to do with drama, both in and out of school. Tucker stresses how he 'soaked up' experiences in order to learn 'and was never afraid to experiment'. Tucker also taught a number of other budding actors including Kristian Phillips and David Jones (David Rees Talbot).

Michael's school had, like the Sec, been putting on plays since the 1920s. *She Stoops to Conquer* had been their first production back in 1926, and after the war they had done a number of Gilbert and Sullivan productions. Oscar Wilde's *The Importance of Being Earnest* was also a popular play locally. This play had already been the first of the annual productions at St Joseph's, the local Roman Catholic Comprehensive, which had opened in 1964. Now the play was performed at Glan Afan with Michael in it. He also set his sights on the most prestigious drama facility in the area: WGYTC. It encompassed a much

wider area than his home town and included Neath and Swansea.

Michael first auditioned for WGYTC when he was twelve. He didn't get in then but was successful the following year and soon, as his father put it, 'He was immersed in it. It was as though he had found his niche.' The first proper play he saw was Arthur Miller's *The Crucible*. This powerful drama had a profound effect on the teenager. He and other members found themselves part of a community dominated by people dedicated to drama and believing in every aspect of theatre production, paying as much attention to technicians as to those in the limelight. Indeed, Michael was initially accepted as a technician. The ethos was one that instilled strict discipline and absolute dedication but in a nurturing and creative educational context.

The first play that Michael performed in was Karel and Josef Čapek's *The Insect Play* (1921) in the 1982–3 season. Michael was an ant. It was, as he has put it, 'hardly a splashy theatre debut but it gave me an opportunity to observe and learn'. He remained with WGYTC until 1988–9, by which time he was at RADA.

Everyone I have interviewed who has been part of this Youth Theatre has acknowledged that it has been transformative. Ken Tucker also taught Matthew Rees (stage name Rhys Matthews)[188] at Glan Afan. Although at first more interested in rugby than drama, thanks to the school production he embraced drama and now teaches at college level. He too went to WGYTC before taking his place at RADA. He comments, 'I think it changed my life. It opened doors to show me – *this* is the profession'. For Francine Morgan who was there in the early days, 'It seemed a bit like some magic fairy tale'.

The roll call of names attached to WGYTC over the years, whether acting, directing or on the technical side, speaks for itself. One Sandfields pupil who went there was Henri Oguike, of Nigerian-Welsh origin. A dancer who has become a leading

musical choreographer, his work is a set piece for A level dance. There are international figures such as the television producer and screenwriter Russell T. Davies and writer, director and producer Ed Thomas. Michael Sheen has even suggested that West Glamorgan has quite possibly 'produced more actors and theatre technicians than any other area in the world'. He told me that there are no comparable facilities of such calibre in Los Angeles.

Just as the voice of Rosalie Mahoney changed and became emotional once Philip Burton's name was mentioned, so the name of Godfrey Evans has a marked effect on those who have come into his orbit. Their faces light up and they are at pains to say how much they owe him. Perhaps the greatest compliment comes from Michael Sheen who simply says that: 'He is the reason for my career and also my work ethos and connection to my community.'

Evans retired in 1992, although he has remained intrinsically connected to WGYTC and enjoys being invited back to help with recent productions.[189] In a sense Michael Sheen and those early members have never quite left either. The loyalty the company has engendered has seen many eminent former students make comebacks. Nick Evans, one of the artistic directorate that took over the running of WGYTC in 2000 (and a former student) returned recently, fresh from directing musicals across the world, to direct a production (with Evans) of *Anne Boleyn* at Pontardawe Arts Centre.

Michael Sheen, like Richard Jenkins and Anthony Hopkins, had found both an institution and someone to encourage and nurture his talent. Unlike his illustrious predecessors, however, he also inherited a family tradition of performance. When he took part in Radio 3's series *Private Passions* about the music that has influenced him, he spoke about how natural acting was for him. 'It was', he said, 'just something that I realised worked in my family.' At family gatherings his great-aunt Marian would

mimic a character. There was 'a currency' in doing some kind of performance.[190]

Showmanship goes a long way back in this family. Mary Ann Blower (née North), Michael's great-great- great-grandmother[191] on his father's side, was from a family of travellers and became Britain's first female lion tamer. Her husband Charles (originally from Denbighshire) was a Shakespearean actor and theatrical agent, but by the early 1890s he was a 'Travelling Showman'.

Later in the decade the Blowers travelled to the United States with Bostock and Wombwell's Travelling Menagerie. Frank Bostock was a renowned showman known as the 'Lion King'. They put on a popular new show in New York and toured the country. Mary Ann's reputation as a lion tamer grew. There are also unsubstantiated claims that she worked with hyenas and wolves. She was, it seems, horribly mauled by a lion but carried on working. Curiously, given the places that Michael Sheen has lived in, after returning from America the couple and at least six children lived on a caravan site in the Maindee area of Newport, Monmouthshire. By 1911 Mary Ann was living in Fairfield, Aberavon. She seems to have run a market stall. When she died in 1923 she was buried in the town.[192] Her daughter Elizabeth Florence Blower married Thomas Henry Sheen, whose father was a travelling showman descended from an Irish family (the family name was sometimes spelt as Sheehan).

Michael's great-grandfather chaired the Port Talbot and District Operatic Society and was a church choirmaster.[193] His grandfather followed in his footsteps, acting in and chairing the Operatic Society. Michael's father, Meyrick, has been involved with the Society since he was fourteen and now, in turn, chairs it. When Michael was only six weeks old, Meyrick brought him on stage at Llantarnam School in Cwmbran for a photograph. Meyrick was playing the part of General Birabeau in a dress rehearsal for the Cwmbran Operatic Society's production of *The*

Desert Song. As a schoolboy Michael also had a part in *The Wizard of Oz*.

Long before Michael discovered WGYTC, his father spotted an opportunity for his son to join him on stage with a part of his own. Meyrick Sheen was taking part in an amateur production of *Camelot*, Lerner and Loewe's musical based on T. H. White's Arthurian story *The Once and Future King* (1958). Richard Burton had starred as King Arthur on Broadway in 1960 and won a Tony Award the following year for best performance in a musical.

The rather less lavish *Camelot* in which Michael had a part was performed at Melyncryddan, a district of Neath. Its amateur operatic society dated back to the 1920s. A young boy was needed to play the part of Tom of Warwick, so Meyrick (who was a knight in the production) suggested the twelve-year-old Michael. He had his first audition and won the part. Michael remembers little about this but it did introduce him to the stage and provide a taste of rehearsals and performance. Tom is a crucial symbolic figure who reminds Arthur of the dreams he held dear as a young man. He is sent forth to disseminate the chivalric ideals of Camelot and ensure that they live on in the future.

Meyrick Sheen is a natural performer and for more than twenty-five years has carved out a subsidiary career as a professional Jack Nicholson lookalike. Employed by a professional agency, he has worked across Britain and travelled to fifteen countries in this guise, covering bar mitzvahs, weddings, commercials, promotional events for businesses, charity events and much else. He and a Sean Connery lookalike from nearby have been much in demand. Sheen Senior has acted since he was young. He found his forte not on the stage but in playing a role that draws upon his resemblance to the actor and enables a naturally gregarious and extrovert personality to flourish.

So Michael Sheen is not the only one in his family to play the

part of a living person. However, his engagement with figures such as Tony Blair, William Masters or David Frost is not, of course, an impersonation (which involves copying behaviour and appearance) but is instead based on a deeper and focused prior study of the psychology of an individual and an internalisation of what appears to drive him. Rather than trying to be *like* the character he is playing, he seeks to inhabit and be that person by playing himself *through* that character. It takes some time to research and prepare: filming the part of Kenneth Williams in *Fantabuloso* only took seventeen days, but preparing for it involved months. Much of what interests Michael in interpreting a part is understanding and probing the disjuncture between how an individual appears on the surface and the demons and conflicts that they battle with internally.[194]

Although Michael's sister followed her father rather than her brother and went into personnel work, his cousin Caroline, six years his junior, is a musical actor who was in the stage and film versions of *Les Misérables*.[195] She is, however, from Gwent, although her parents hailed from Port Talbot and met at Dyffryn School where they were both acting in one of Selwyn Davies' productions.

Another relative is Michael Conway from Margam, who was inspired to go on the stage after seeing Michael in the Royal Shakespeare Company's *Henry V* at Stratford-upon-Avon in 1997.[196] Conway works in musical theatre and covered all the leads in *The Jersey Boys* in London's West End from 2009. And there is even a link by marriage between Richard Burton and Michael Sheen. Michael's great aunt-in-law Doris (Caroline Sheen's grandmother) was a second cousin of Elfed James.

Aged sixteen, Michael Sheen joined the National Youth Theatre of Wales. One of his contemporaries there was Helen John (not a relative of mine) from Sandfields Comprehensive, who later became a teacher of Drama there. She remembers the Youth Theatre doing a production of *Godspell*, for which they

engaged two professional actors to be Jesus and Judas in the mistaken belief that none of the youngsters could tackle these roles. Michael was cast as a sheep. In the parable of the Prodigal Son the sheep had to move up and down and across scaffolding and, as Helen John tells it, 'He absolutely milked it. All the audience were talking about was the sheep.' He had learned how to upstage.

Despite his discovery of the stage at a young age, Michael initially planned to do a university degree. He studied English, Drama and Sociology at A level at Neath College and was offered a place to study English and Drama at Warwick University. His love of English literature and language seems to have come from his mother Irene. Her ancestors include Michael's great-grandfather John James Price, a collier-preacher and autodidact who penned his own autobiography. He had been born in 1893 just a couple of miles from Pontrhydyfen and attended the same chapel as the family of Richard Burton.

Although he began work at the Llantwit Colliery Tonmawr (with his father and eldest brother) *before* his thirteenth birthday, Price's autobiography is a very articulate and moving account.[197] His mother died the day he received his first pay packet. Like Michael he was a good sportsman. He became a champion walker after winning a twelve-mile walk from Port Talbot to Bridgend (fourteen supporters' coaches were provided from Port Talbot alone).[198] But competitive walking resulted in the excessive drinking which had also blighted his father's life. A dramatic conversion, however, saw the young man become a lay preacher. When Michael was Peer Gynt in Ibsen's eponymous play he based his interpretation on such a figure, playing him not as a Norwegian but as a Welshman.[199]

Michael's experience at WGYTC gradually persuaded him that he wanted a career in the theatre and that drama school would be more appropriate than university. He left school in

1987 and took a 'gap' year. Rather than travelling the world, he worked in a local burger bar. This gave him cash and it was handy for acting at WGYTC. But the Port Talbot that Michael was now working in was very different from the town that Anthony Hopkins had known when he had left school. Burger Master was its first drive-through takeaway, a somewhat makeshift affair on the dual carriageway in Baglan. Burgers would become only too prominent in the town's landscape as it and its fortunes were reshaped. In 1976 the Aberafan shopping centre had opened, dislocating the town's retail hub Station Road and starting a process that would turn it into a street of fast food outlets.

The Port Talbot that Michael worked in still had its steelworks but the number of steelworkers had been dramatically reduced. Structural problems had existed in the British steel industry for some years, with too many steelworks of insufficient size. This was most evident during periods of privatisation when competition was rife and sites were pitted against each other.

According to Stephen Parry, an expert on the history of the industry in the Port Talbot area in the twentieth century, after denationalising steel the Conservative government's decision in the late fifties to build new strip mills at Llanwern and Ravenscraig, but not at the Abbey Works, challenged Port Talbot's role as the leading strip mill.[200] As early as 1960 considerable over-manning was evident at Port Talbot and as competition grew and profits fell (from 1960 onwards) so this became more acute. The first attempts to reduce numbers were seen in the mid-sixties. The Steel Company of Wales ceased to exist in 1967, but although renationalisation led to the amalgamation of fourteen UK steel companies by the new British Steel Corporation (BSC), the workforce was still well over 16,000.[201]

It was in the 1970s when Michael was at secondary school

that the town's problems became really apparent. The oil crisis of 1973–4, international competition and a global decline in the demand for steel were accompanied by a recession at home that hit the motor trade badly and hastened the decline in the demand for steel. One overdue and highly significant development, however, was the opening in 1970 of a new purpose-built tidal harbour for the town. Fully laden ore carriers of up to 100,000 tons (ten times the previous capacity) could now be berthed.[202] It cost £20 million to build the harbour but dependence on foreign ores and the need for the Works to make the most of its advantageous coastal location meant that it was money well spent, helping to ensure the survival of the Port Talbot steel industry and making the town Britain's first major ore terminal.

In 1978–9, just before Margaret Thatcher became Prime Minister, BSC losses at Port Talbot totalled more than £30 million.[203] There was investment in the works but soon there were rumours not only of job losses but also of possible closure. In 1980 a three-month national strike followed Sir Keith Joseph's announcement of a wage freeze. Industrial relations did not look like improving with the appointment of the intransigent Ian MacGregor as BSC's new chairman, but union action over cuts was tempered at Port Talbot by fears that the Works might close altogether and, rather than confrontation, an uneasy compliance ensued. During the year that Michael worked in the town MacGregor carried out his brief to privatise BSC.[204] The mid-eighties saw a new strip mill and a concast plant – more than £500 million were invested during the decade – but by 1988, when Michael left for college, the number of Port Talbot steelworkers had been reduced to 4,689, roughly a quarter of the size of twenty years earlier.

Michael won places at eight drama schools. He chose RADA and thrived there. Lloyd Trott, who taught him there, remembers that:

Such was Michael's proven versatility and theatrical stamina by the end of his second (of three) years at RADA that I could happily assign two very contrasting roles to perform in scenes in the same class on the same day, 22nd June 1990. The roles were Valentin Arregui, the imprisoned Brazilian revolutionary in Manuel Puig's *The Kiss of the Spiderwoman*, and Curly Delafield, the existential, ethically ambiguous investigator in David Hare's *Knuckle*, set in Guildford, parodying film noir and American thrillers.

Michael won a Laurence Olivier Bursary (providing funding for exceptional students) in his final year.[205] As a student he shared a house with two Welsh friends, Jason Hughes and Hywel Simons. Both had grown up in nearby Porthcawl and become LAMDA students. Michael had first met them during his summer stints with National Youth Theatre Wales in Cardiff. Before graduating in 1991, he won the part of the Greek piano-playing prodigy Alexandros Eliopolos in *When She Danced* at London's Globe Theatre. The star was Vanessa Redgrave, whose mesmerising portrayal of Isadora Duncan was much praised. Nevertheless, Michael Billington noted Michael's subtle performance.[206]

The following year Michael played Romeo in Gregory Horsov's production of *Romeo and Juliet* at Manchester's Royal Exchange Theatre. It then toured. He was nominated for a M.E.N. Theatre Award from the *Manchester Evening News* for Best Actor for this performance. It won plaudits from the influential *Observer* theatre critic Michael Coveney, who declared that Michael had 'burst forth' as the most exciting young actor of his generation'.[207] This 'lanky, elfin, volatile, electrifying and fearless young actor' invited comparison with Nicol Williamson and Jonathan Pryce. He was, Coveney added, 'markedly Welsh, with a strong vibrant voice and a devilish, saturnine demeanour'. His portrayal of the 'mad, mercurial

side' of Romeo was unsurpassed and Coveney applauded the way in which he and Kate Byers (Juliet) had enabled Shakespeare to be appreciated by a contemporary audience. A couple of years later, in anticipation of Sheen's *Peer Gynt*, Coveney declared that 'Sheen will surely have staying power'. In an interesting use of a nationality as an adjective, he added that he was 'quick, Welsh, mercurial and just 25 years old'.[208]

All of this presaged a hugely successful career on stage and screen, littered with memorable performances, numerous awards and international fame. Yet, as we shall see in Part Two, for many of those from Port Talbot, Michael Sheen's crowning achievement to date has been his creation and realisation of *The Passion*, a site-specific three-day performance across the town at Easter 2011 for which he and his co-director Bill Mitchell would win the Theatre Awards UK prize for Best Director.

PART TWO

IN THEIR FOOTSTEPS
and
GIVING BACK

4

Products of Port Talbot

'You've got Hopkins, me, Richard Burton and Sheen' declares an expansive Rob Brydon in the BBC television series *The Trip* (2010).[209] He and Steve Coogan, masters of improvisational comedy, are tucking into yet another gourmet meal on their talking and dining trip round northern England where they are 'playing with perceptions of ourselves' and 'exaggerating things you might half feel.'[210] 'The Port Talbot Four. That's what we're known as' Brydon brags, before launching into another of his impersonations of the Port Talbot stars (especially Anthony Hopkins) that punctuate the episodes and are guaranteed to evoke a less than appreciative response from Coogan.[211]

Rob Brydon may be joking, but he definitely qualifies as one of the Port Talbot elite. He demonstrates too the importance of legacy and, as a popular and talented contemporary performer – star of a play at London's Old Vic in 2015 – he is a significant figure amongst the fifty Port Talbot actors listed in the Appendix. The careers of a selection of these actors are highlighted in this chapter in mini-biographies that suggest the wide range of roles and skills they have deployed and continue to display.

Since 2010 Brydon has been immortalised in the now tranquil Afan Valley alongside Richard Burton and Dick Wagstaff, former Head Ranger at Afan Forest Park. Represented as steel silhouettes next to a wooden bench, they were the top three choices in a local community poll run by Sustrans'

national Portrait Bench project. Cyclists and walkers encounter them on the Richard Burton trail.[212]

Rob Brydon hails from Baglan like Michael Sheen, who is a couple of years younger, and the stand-up comedian and writer Lloyd Langford (a former WGYTC student described by the *Guardian* as 'one of the sharpest comedic minds on the circuit').[213] Brydon's father, a car dealer, came from the same Margam street as Anthony Hopkins. His mother sang in local operettas.

Robert Brydon Jones was, however, born in Swansea and although he lived in Port Talbot, his early education was in private schools in Porthcawl, then Swansea (where he attended the same school as Catherine Zeta Jones). His family then moved for a time to nearby Porthcawl where he went to the local comprehensive. Here he flourished, thanks to the inspirational Roger Burnell, a trained actor who taught drama and put on annual musicals such as *Carousel* in which Brydon played the lead role of Billy Bigelow. The talented actress and writer Ruth Jones, his future co-star in *Gavin and Stacey*, two years below him, was in the same production and they became friends.[214] Another former pupil is now a familiar face on television and stage: the *Game of Thrones* and *Stella* star Owen Teale. He grew up close to Margam in North Cornelly.[215]

In his autobiography Brydon reflects on his unsuccessful applications to London drama schools. With characteristic self-deprecation he comments that 'the whole business of coming to London in the hope that the schools would recognise they had the next Richard Burton on their doorstep was destined to be a failure'. It was, in a sense, a burden as well as a boon.

Brydon felt that he was out of place auditioning at Central and RADA, sensing in other candidates a seriousness and concern with acting as 'an art form that could explore the human condition'.[216] Since childhood he has wanted to entertain and make people laugh. In this sense he follows in the

tradition of Port Talbot's comedian Ossie Morris.[217] Yet the double-edged, complex nature of many of the characters Rob Brydon has created demonstrates that, despite his earlier misgivings, he *has* also explored 'the human condition' in his work.

Brydon went to the Welsh College of Music and Drama in 1984, the year that Richard Burton died. Hanging on the wall in his digs was a magazine photograph of the actor in the Broadway production of *Hamlet* twenty years earlier. As a student he attended (standing throughout) the 'stupendously good performance' by Anthony Hopkins in *Pravda* at London's National Theatre, pronouncing it the 'finest piece of theatre' he had seen.[218] Hopkins remains a hero for him: 'one of the greatest film and stage actors of our time or any time … a genius actor with great craft as well'.[219]

Brydon is well aware that:

> Two different generations had done it – not just one – two people had become world famous… it's inspiring and it's enabling because you see someone's done it before you and that's important… it gave you confidence knowing that they had come from this small and untrumpeted part of the world… It's such a small place and you only take pride in it.

How different it must be, he remarks, to come from a place where there had been nobody of note. Di Botcher echoes Rob Brydon's words and wonders what it would have been like had there not been a Burton and Hopkins to emulate. She and others maintain that Port Talbot and its schools have been predisposed towards drama due to the fact that there is a reputation to uphold.

Matthew Aubrey, a young actor from Sandfields, remarks: 'It's fascinating – for such a macho town, it's alright to be an actor.' A combination of a rich and long tradition of amateur

dramatics and the knowledge that Richard Burton, miner's son, and Anthony Hopkins, son of a baker, had both made the 'big time' has validated the profession in Port Talbot.

In 1970 an article in *The Times* suggested that 'Somewhere in transit from the thickset shadow of Richard Burton towards the leaping light of Laurence Olivier there simmers a volcano: Anthony Hopkins'.[220] For the latter, the Burton legacy has been, in a sense, double-edged. Here was somebody to emulate and he has admitted that he wanted to be like him. In 1994 Hopkins received an Oscar for *The Silence of the Lambs* and Port Talbot granted him the Freedom of the Borough of Port Talbot. In his acceptance speech he recalled his weekly art lessons with his teacher Bernice Evans in Station Road. As he was painting a pilot in poster colours her boyfriend arrived to take her to see *Odd Man Out* at the Plaza. Hopkins recalls how, on that golden summer evening, in strode a striking young man. Bernice introduced him and said 'This is Richard. He's going to be an actor'. It was, of course, Richard Burton. Apparently the young Hopkins was suitably impressed and decided that he wanted to be like the actor.

In the early days of Hopkins' career it was, however, difficult to escape Richard Burton, especially since at times their lifestyles as well as their superb voices invariably invited comparison. Quentin Falk calls him Anthony Hopkins' 'constant spectre'.[221] Another biographer claims that by 1957 Hopkins was being dubbed 'Young Dick Burton' by Taibach neighbours, a soubriquet he loathed.[222] Yet it seems unlikely that local people, well aware that Rich was how Burton was known, would have used the name Dick.

Burton and Hopkins had been the only ones in their families to date to become actors. Both were blessed with unforgettable voices and prodigious memories. Burton delighted especially in his ability to quote at will from Shakespeare.[223] Doug Rees remembers how, at the civic reception for Hopkins' Freedom of

the Borough, he quoted to him Rees' own lines from the play *Outward Bound* performed at the YMCA in 1955. But both Burton and Hopkins were also famously cursed by alcoholism when comparatively young. That tendency towards self-destruction was problematic, though what Michael Sheen calls their 'dark energy' has had a productive side too, stimulating others.

Anthony Hopkins, who knew Burton's first wife Sybil, cast their daughter Kate Burton as Helen in a 1995 film he directed (and acted in) called *August*. Filmed on the Llŷn peninsula, this was Julian Mitchell's reworking of a translation of Chekhov's *Uncle Vanya* in a Welsh setting.[224] It may, at first sight, appear surprising that Hopkins had only met her father Richard Burton a few times. A few years after his encounter at the art class Hopkins called at Caradoc Street and got the actor's autograph. In fact there was a connection through marriage between the two families. Burton's brother-in-law Elfed James, who had raised him with his wife Cis, had a cousin on his father's side who married into the Phillips family. Anthony Hopkins' maternal grandmother had been a member of this family, and his name Philip Anthony Hopkins was a genuflection to what was also his mother's maiden name.

Many years later the two actors met on Broadway. Hopkins starred in 1974 as the psychiatrist in Peter Shaffer's *Equus*. Anthony Perkins followed him in this role and then Burton took over. The two men with their Taibach memories met briefly backstage. Burton called at Hopkins's dressing room and Hopkins returned the compliment when Burton was in the play.

But they never worked together. And this should not come as a surprise. Was there really room for both of them in the same place? Despite their very different styles the world had lumped them together and they both seem to have preferred to respect each other's space. Only in 1988, a few years after Burton's death, did the fifty-year-old Anthony Hopkins play First Voice

in a complete recording of *Under Milk Wood*, the first since Burton's memorable BBC recording in 1954. The new version was for an EMI musical album put together by the Beatles' former producer George Martin.[225]

Michael Sheen celebrates his Port Talbot predecessors. He feels that Richard Burton and Anthony Hopkins 'made acting acceptable for sports-mad boys'.[226] In 2010 he presented a radio programme called 'The Richard Burton Legacy', in which he described the actor's voice as 'one of the great voices of the twentieth century'.[227] The programme included an interview with Burton's great-nephew Guy Masterson. The son of Cis and Elfed's daughter Marian, he had been born in London (as Guy Mastroianni) in 1961, but retained strong Welsh connections. An actor and prolific director and producer, he directed Mark Jenkins' one-man show *Playing Burton*, which toured the UK and New Zealand in the 1990s.

When quizzed about which British actor he most admires, Sheen cites the 'embarassment of riches' provided by his hometown, loyally mentioning Burton and Hopkins. He has also commented on how Burton's acting taught him a lot about 'the different ways to deliver power'.[228]

Sheen has played a number of roles made famous by the actor. For example, he was Jimmy Porter in *Look Back in Anger* at the Royal Exchange in Manchester in 1995 then in 1999, earning nominations for both a Laurence Olivier Award and an Evening Standard for Best Actor (in a drama that he had first studied at O level). The *Independent* declared that although he had 'cornered the market in explosive energy' this was his finest performance to date.[229] Sheen felt that he learned from the way in which Richard Burton 'reined in' his anger in his portrayal of the character in the film of John Osborne's play.[230] In this production Sheen's old flatmate Jason Hughes (best known as Sergeant Jones in television's *Midsomer Murders*) played Cliff, Jimmy Porter's flatmate. Peter Stead pronounced it 'one of the

theatrical events of the year' adding that 'For the first time since Brando, an actor in a vest was the era's dramatic icon'.[231] The morning after his opening night in *Hamlet* Sheen unveiled a plaque to Burton at the house in Lyndhurst Road, Hampstead where he had lived with Sybil.

When Michael Sheen participated in Radio 3's *Private Passions,* one of his musical selections was the opening of Jeff Wayne's musical version of *The War of the Worlds*, featuring Burton's voice.[232] And in the same year, the centenary of Dylan Thomas's birth, Sheen had two opportunities to follow Burton's vocal repertoire via performances of *Under Milk Wood.*[233]

The first was in a shortened television version for BBC Wales.[234] Its imaginative casting included Tom Jones as Captain Cat and Bryn Terfel personifying the musical nation through his Reverend Eli Jenkins. Sheen was the First Voice (doing his recording from the States). He won the approval of Gary Raymond in the *Wales Arts Review*, who saw it as confirmation that he was the 'only heir' for the 'Burton/Hopkins throne'.[235] For Sheen, Burton's recording was one of the greatest pieces ever produced by the BBC on radio or television.[236]

Then, on 26 October 2014, on the eve of the centenary of Dylan Thomas's birth, Sheen directed and acted in the play at the 92nd Street 'Y' (YMCA) Theatre in Manhattan.[237] This was where Dylan Thomas had done the first read-through of his brand new 'Play for Voices' shortly before he died in 1953. Thomas had completed the final lines just hours before the event. As at this original reading, there were only six actors involved. Each read several parts sitting in a semi-circle. Sheen had chosen for his centenary version Richard Burton's actor daughter Kate (whose mother played Myfanwy Price in the famous recording in 1954), and Port Talbot's Matthew Aubrey and Francine Morgan were also in Sheen's select cast. Sheen had studied the play in school and at WGYTC and was highly conscious of the false over-familiarity that can accompany such

a well-known piece. He was also keen to bring together Welsh and American audiences, and the event was broadcast live on BBC Radio Wales at the same time as the audience in New York watched and heard the reading.

Burton's Shakespearean and other stage roles have clearly had an impact on Michael Sheen and reviewers cannot resist citing the Burton-Hopkins lineage. Not surprisingly, Sheen recognises the expectations this can create and that, though a source of pride, it can be demanding. As he stressed in Paul Islwyn Lewis' excellent 1998 documentary about his career to date (set in large part in Port Talbot and with Sheen reciting lines from his recent stage work): 'I'm the new Michael Sheen not the next Richard Burton.'[238]

Sheen's teenage love of cinema had not encompassed the work of Burton and Hopkins. Instead he devoured old black and white movies on television on Sunday afternoons and enjoyed watching the drama critic Kenneth Tynan on the *South Bank Show*.[239] Anthony Hopkins had seen Burton in *The Robe* but by the time Sheen was going to the Plaza (those other cinemas so beloved of the earlier stars had already closed), it was new films like *Star Wars* and *Grease* that he was enjoying. The legend of Richard Burton had, however, remained pervasive, as had the manifold stories of a larger than life character. As for Anthony Hopkins, it was only in 2007 that Sheen met him. As we shall see here and in the next chapter, the immense talent and fame of both of the superstars has left an indelible print on the town as well as on the aspirations of its people.

A Port Talbot-born actor who was compared with Richard Burton – and with Gary Cooper – was the matinée idol Ronald Lewis. Born in 1928, just three years after Richard Burton and dying two years before him, Lewis lived in the town until he was seven, when he moved with his family to London. The war years saw him evacuated back to south Wales and Bridgend

Grammar School (where he played Bassanio in the school production of *The Merchant of Venice*). His decision to become an actor was apparently as a result of seeing Shaw's *Saint Joan* at the Prince of Wales Theatre in Cardiff. He then headed for RADA.

Lewis' first professional role was in Oscar Wilde's *An Ideal Husband* in 1950 in repertory at Worthing. His film debut came three years later as a boxer in *The Square Ring* (after playing in it on stage at the Lyric, Hammersmith). According to the *South Wales Echo and Express*, 'handsome, tall, manly' Ronald Lewis 'took London by storm' in 1955 in Peter Hall's production of Eugene O'Neill's *Mourning Becomes Electra* at the Arts Theatre Club in Great Newport Street.[240] This was followed by a starring role opposite Vivien Leigh in Noel Coward's musical *South Sea Bubble*.

Although he continued on the stage, he now spent much of his time making films for Ealing and Alexander Korda's London Films. He made more than two dozen films in the fifties and sixties. He was in *The Prisoner* (1955) with Alec Guinness and Jack Hawkins and in Peter Ustinov's *Billy Budd* (1962). His repertoire was wide: from comedies such as *Sailor Beware!* (1956) to Hammer Horror. But his personal life also became something of a horror story.

During the run of *Peter Pan* in the West End, Lewis' wife alleged that he had assaulted her.[241] He failed to appear in court and a warrant was issued for his arrest. He could no longer get work and although he still did some television, a bit part in *Z Cars* in 1978 marked his final television appearance. He was drinking heavily.

He was to be First Voice in a production of *Under Milk Wood* at Theatr Gwynedd in 1975. The Pontrhydyfen actor Siân Owen was stage manager and Jennifer Hill from Margam was in the cast (she had acted in the Port Talbot Drama Club in the 1950s before training at LAMDA). As the curtain was about to go up on the first night, Ronnie Lewis lay prostrate on the stage. He

had ceased drinking in preparation for the part but the tension of it all had caused him to fit and prompted a heart attack. He was resuscitated and taken to hospital. In 1981 he was declared bankrupt with debts of £21,188. Just months later in January 1982, he took a fatal overdose. His body was discovered in a cheap boarding house in Pimlico. He was fifty-three.

Another contemporary was John Morgan Rees, who also had a tragic end – and a sad start.[242] He was born in Port Talbot in 1927, one of three children. After his father was revealed as a bigamist and went to prison, Rees was put in a local orphanage. Some time later his mother took the children to Cardiff. He did National Service, becoming a renowned army boxer, then trained at Central. In 1954 he was in repertory theatre at Derby Playhouse. He lived in the same digs as John Osborne and his first wife Pamela, who rented an attic room. The three became friends and on Sunday evenings they would share a meal, read the papers and listen to music together. Osborne (descended on his father's side from several generations of Newportians) was writing *Look Back in Anger* and the character of the young working class Welshman Cliff Lewis was based in large part on Rees. Certainly the play's opening scene conjured up the digs in Derby. Three years later, to help the couple gain a divorce, Rees agreed to be co-respondent even though he had not had an affair with Pamela.

Rees did not appear in the play or film of Osborne's famous work but he was in the cast of six in Peter Gill's gritty drama *The Sleepers Den*, set in the playwright's hometown of Cardiff. He became a close friend of Harold Pinter's and played Aston in a television production of *The Caretaker* and toured America in this. Rees appeared in a number of films including Andrew Sinclair's *Under Milk Wood* starring Richard Burton. A serious scholar of German – he had made several films in East Germany in the fifties – and of horse riding, he died in Spain in 1994 during a riding holiday. He is buried in Motril. When his family

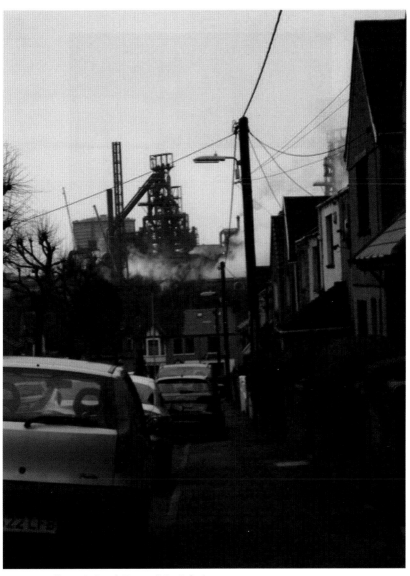

1. Port Talbot: A Steel Town (Nia John)

2. Philip Burton in the YMCA's *Othello*,
June 1932 (Newark Lewis)

3. Philip Burton: The Schoolmaster (Dyffryn School Archives)

4. Richard Burton and Meredith Jones (the James family)

5. T. Owen Jones (Dyffryn School Archives)

6. Richard Burton (Siân Owen)

SEPTEMBER, 1940

9 MONDAY Played football at blind side wing forward. I am wondering whether he intends keeping me in that position. I hope so. Tom Mainwaring is back in school again. Played football with us. Pretty good too.

10 TUESDAY I intended stopping in and doing homework but Phillips came and sent a little boy up later, so I went with him. Phillips did not come in until 6 o'clock tonight. It is very annoying. London bombed fiercely for but—

11 WEDNESDAY School as usual except that we are having films by gas companies and food notes etc which are not very interesting but offer a relieve from the monotony of school life. Mr Button says there is a long new film coming.

Sunset 7.23 p.m. at Greenwich. (See below for approximate Provincial Time).
Light Lamps 1 hour after Sunset.

Birmingham, add 9 min. | Manchester, add 13 min. | Glasgow, add 25 min. | Dublin, add 29 min.

98

SEPTEMBER, 1940

12 THURSDAY This morning Stanley Jones gave me a letter from Edie. Inside it was another letter from Will. It contained half a crown. That night I went to the Gnoll and did not tell Sis. It was quite a good show starring Richard Green and Dix.

13 FRIDAY This morning the milkboy told Sis that he had seen me in the Gnoll eating chocolates etc but I denied it and she believed me—at least I think so—although it was no crime. We had Button today—very interesting talk on Essays.

14 SATURDAY Fetched 6 pints of blackberries this morning and I sold them all. The sale realized 1/6 each for Sis & I. Went to Regent in the night—it was pretty good. Unckle Charles gave me 6d. I am not going to get papers for aunt Ede again.

15 SUNDAY *17th Sunday after Trinity* Determined to work hard at school and break all records by passing matric 1st time. Very few Vox boys have ever done it.

99

7. Richard Jenkins' handwritten diary, 9–15 September 1940 (© Sally Burton, Richard Burton Archives, Swansea University)

8. Port Talbot Secondary School (Dyffryn School Archives)

9. Richard Jenkins (third from left in back row) and class in 1940 (Dyffryn School Archives)

10. The first autograph? (Dyffryn School Archives)

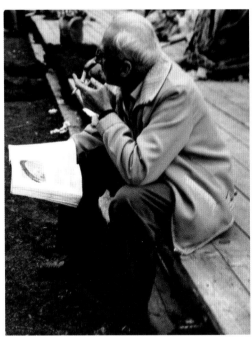

11. Leo Lloyd (Jeff Maddox)

12. Cyril and Clarice Jenkins (Cyril Jenkins Archive)

Y.M.C.A. PLAYERS

Port Talbot Y.M.C.A. Amateur
Dramatic Society

presents

"OUTWARD
BOUND"

by Sutton Vane.

Programme · · · · THREEPENCE.

Officers of the Society.

President	W. IVOR NICHOLAS
Chairman	DUNCAN MILES
Secretary	DOUGLAS KERR
Joint Stage Managers	ANTHONY HOPKINS, DUNCAN MILES
Wardrobe	WALTER DAVIES
Technical Adviser	GEORGE HARWOOD
Make-up	W. IVOR NICHOLAS
Property Mistress	Miss MARGARET MORGAN

— END —

We gratefully acknowledge the invaluable assistance rendered to the Society in this production by—
Talbach & Port Talbot Co-operative Society (for the Loan of Furniture); Mr. George Penn, Grand Hotel; Y.M.C.A. Camera Club; Mr. Emlyn Spices, Station Road; Alex Brice, Ltd.; and Mr. Bryn Thomas.

13. Programme for *Outward Bound* 1955 with Anthony Hopkins as Joint Stage Manager. Notice the advertisement for the family bakery (Cyril Jenkins Archive)

14. Portrait of Anthony Hopkins by Roy Guy in Port Talbot YMCA (© Roy Guy)

15. Anthony Hopkins (Tony) expresses his gratitude to Cyril Jenkins
(Anthony Hopkins, Cyril Jenkins Archive)

16. The young Godfrey Evans as Becket in Selwyn Davies' school production (Dyffryn School Archives)

17. 'Once in a Lifetime', WGYTC production, 1985. Maxine Evans, Darren Lawrence (Port Talbot), Karen Willans, Michael Sheen (Port Talbot), Buddug Morgan (Kevin Matherick)

18. Dennis Burgess (Peter Stevens)

19. Ivor Emmanuel (the Emmanuel family)

20. Robert Blythe (Robert Blythe)

21. Di Botcher (Di Botcher)

22. Rob Brydon (Trevor Leighton)

23. Siân Owen and her uncle Richard Burton (Angela V. John)

24. The Portrait Bench on the Richard Burton Trail: Richard Burton, Rob Brydon and Forest Ranger Dick Wagstaff (Siân Owen)

25. Norman Comer (Norman Comer)

26. Godfrey Evans, founder of WGYTC at its 40th anniversary celebrations in Port Talbot, 2015 (Godfrey Evans/ WGYTC)

27. Glan Afan School Centenary production of *Under Milk Wood*, 1996. Professional actors and ex-pupils Michael Sheen and Norman Comer played 1st and 2nd Voice and local actor/producer Alan Davies was Captain Cat. Ken Tucker was the producer (Ken Tucker)

28. Sandfields School production of *Sweeney Todd* in 2003 with Marc Antolin and Christina Modestou (Helen John)

29. Sandfields School pupils rehearsing with their drama teacher Helen John for *The Wizard of Oz*, 2015 (Sara Mays)

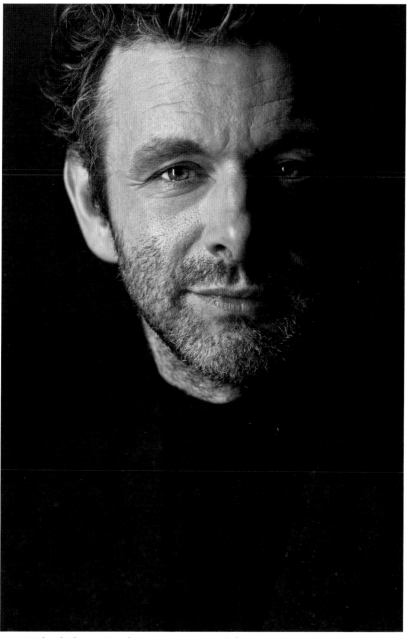

30. Michael Sheen (Sarah Dunn, www.sarahdunn.com)

31. Programme for *Behold The Man* (Carol Scott)

32. Carol Mends (assistant director), Ina D. Jones (producer and director) and Carol Scott (assistant director) attending a planning meeting for *Behold The Man* in Margam Park with Margam Castle in the background (David Scott)

33. *The Passion*: At the Seaside Social Club on the Saturday Night: Kyle Rees, Matthew Woodyatt, Francine Morgan, Michael Sheen, David Rees Talbot, Matthew Aubrey, John-Paul Macleod, Darren Lawrence. All these actors are from Port Talbot with the exception of Gwent's Matthew Woodyatt (Richard Hardcastle/National Theatre Wales)

34. *The Passion*: Michael Sheen as The Teacher in the crowd (Geraint Lewis/National Theatre Wales)

35. *The Passion*: Members of the Company on the Beach (Richard Hardcastle/National Theatre Wales

were clearing out his London home they found on the doormat a letter from the daughter he had never known saying she thought he was her father. Her mother had put her up for adoption and she later emigrated to Australia. She took her own life just two years after her father's death.

Ronald Lewis' links with Port Talbot did not remain strong and Rees' connections were tenuous. There have, however, been many others who, although they never reached the dizzy heights of its biggest stars, have also taken to the big and small screen as well as the stage, sometimes combining it with other jobs. They were intrinsically linked with the support for drama that was evident in the town. The first batch of these professional and semi-professional actors were contemporaries of Richard Jenkins at the Sec but are best understood as products of the Philip Burton drama stable.

They include Dennis Burgess, an imposing figure who towers above his classmates in school photographs. He taught locally and was with the YMCA Players until 1955, then joined the Wayfarers. Eventually, thanks to Richard Burton, he became a professional actor (see Chapter 5).

There was Brinley Jenkins who taught for seven years, combining this with radio drama in Cardiff where he worked for his former teacher Philip Burton, now a BBC features producer. Burton recognised Jenkins' ability but advised him to stick to teaching unless 'you are completely burned up with a desire to make acting your career'.[243] He was. He took a drama course at Caerleon Training College then joined the BBC Welsh Repertory Company in 1953 (earning £9 weekly) acting in hundreds of Welsh and English radio programmes.

Evan Morgan was another keen student of drama who became a schoolmaster. He was seen as the foundation stone of the Wayfarers and was secretary of the Thespian Players. He also wrote plays and acted for the BBC in radio and television part-time.

Another member of this group was Catherine Dolan, known as Phyllis. She was Richard Burton's first girlfriend and had acted with him in *Pygmalion* at school. The local paper praised her diction.[244] She went to RADA and worked in radio and television (appearing in *Armchair Theatre* in the early 1960s) as well as touring in plays in Europe and the United States.[245]

The leading lady in the Sec plays in the early 1940s had been Dilys Jones. She is an example of those whose passion remained theatre, yet whose main career was not acting.[246] She taught infants. She was from a strict chapel-going family and her mother not keen on the idea of her daughter going on the stage. It had been bad enough when she had uttered the word 'bloody' in *Pygmalion* in 1943 (the *Port Talbot Guardian* had noted how Philip Burton's production had 'no blue pencil censorship').[247] But Dilys Jones carried on acting for her former school and the BBC, especially in radio programmes for children, blurring the edges between professional and amateur theatre. She even had a tiny part in Burton's first film *The Last Days of Dolwyn*. A friend has recalled how much drama mattered to her: 'The minute you crossed her threshold you were on the stage.'

The town's key role models for acting have been male. Nevertheless, in 1941 (when Wales had the highest percentage of female war workers in Britain) the *Port Talbot Guardian* ran an article entitled 'How to Be a Film Star. Advice for Local Talent'. It paid tribute to the provision of facilities for amateur dramatics in the area, pointing out that numerous successful productions had revealed 'local stars' who would, 'in the ordinary way, never have been suspected of possessing acting powers'.[248] It was becoming tougher to succeed and it was hoped that 'our local aspirants for stage and film honours will know what is expected of them'. Warning that the demands of technicolour and the modern camera lens were enhancing the need for physical perfection – the article ignored male actors

here, seeing this as relevant for women alone – it asked, 'Can any of our local actresses "make the grade?"'

The paper's appreciation of the community's provision of facilities is worth noting. As we have seen, various drama groups provided a basis for nurturing talent. Many British towns had flourishing drama groups and modestly titled Little Theatres could be found close by, for example in Neath and Porthcawl. And, unlike Port Talbot, which had long since lost its New Theatre in a fire, they usually boasted proper theatres for amateur and professional actors. Not until 1958 did Port Talbot gain a modern large space for performances and then it was part of Sandfields Comprehensive. Only with the Princess Royal Theatre, which opened eleven years later, did the town have its own purpose-built theatre once more.

This, however, had not deterred either the Port Talbot Little Theatre or the Taibach (Young) People's Theatre, from thriving. Leo Lloyd had started the latter in 1958. He died five years later but it carried on with plays by Eynon Evans and Noel Coward, alongside more weighty material by playwrights such as Bertolt Brecht. It no longer exists, but the Little Theatre survives despite having had numerous homes.[249] In November 2014 it put on *Hi-de-Hi!* at the Princess Royal Theatre, directed by Ken Tucker, Michael Sheen's former teacher.

By no means all of the amateur producers and directors were male. Eunice Evans was responsible for the work of Cymdeithas Ddrama Cymrodorion Dyffryn Afan a Margam.[250] Lloyd and the old Port Talbot Drama Club benefitted from the skills of Mrs Wood, and Maggie Lloyd often assisted him. Ina D. Jones was a key figure in both the Port Talbot Little Theatre and, as we shall see, in producing and directing Margam's many Passion Plays, where Carol Mends and Carol Scott were also involved in production.

The life stories of a number of Port Talbot's twentieth-century professional actors show that local amateur theatre was part of

their development. Take Douglas Blackwell. Born in Gloucester in 1924, he grew up in Port Talbot and attended the County School. He became a draughtsman but made his mark locally acting, directing and writing plays. His one-act comedy thriller *Branch Line* was performed by the Wesley Hall Dramatic Society in 1941 (he was a church member) and won first prize at the Pontypridd Youth Eisteddfod the following year.[251] He moved into repertory but it was the development of television that ensured for Blackwell regular work and exposure as a character actor. In 1951 he appeared in *Treasure Island*. This triggered a fifty-year stint on television. He appeared in many of the most popular series of the day, with eleven years of *Z Cars*. He was in films too, including *The Ipcress File* (1965). Douglas Blackwell died in London in 2009 aged eighty-five.

Acting in that 1941 play *Branch Line* and in Port Talbot Drama Club plays was Michael Jones, whose home was in the same street as the Wesley Hall. Another ex-County schoolboy who acted with former pupils, he became an instrument mechanic in the steelworks. He managed to pay his own way through RADA and became an actor, changing his name to Marshall Jones. His work encompassed Shakespeare and 'chillers'.

The career of Norman Comer intersected with a number of Port Talbot actors, amateur and professional. Comer came from Llewellyn Street, half of which was later demolished for the motorway. He was taught in primary school by Evan Morgan and saw him in a play at the YMCA when he was about ten. Like many other children, Comer took part in Sunday School performances, but it was being selected by the BBC for a televised schools debate (with Glan Afan boys and Dyffryn girls) when he was in Glan Afan's fourth form that fired his imagination. He was good at Physics and Keith Jones, his teacher for the subject, also put on the school plays. Jones was yet another lover of drama who had been taught by Philip

Burton at the Sec and now encouraged Comer to join school productions.

Comer began reading Mathematical Physics at Birmingham University but was increasingly drawn to drama. Terry Hands was a fellow student and after he went on to RADA Comer applied too and was accepted there, despite lacking much experience. He left Birmingham part way through his course.

Comer spent many years in English repertory theatre, which he loved. Tall and striking, he also did a lot of television work, and was known as 'Barlow's Right Hand Man' for his part as a Detective Sergeant in 'Barlow at Large'. He worked with Douglas Blackwell in one episode. Later, after completing the degree he had earlier abandoned and getting a postgraduate teaching qualification, Comer returned home and taught Mathematics and Drama in Porthcawl and Bridgend for some years. He did not abandon the stage, acting in both professional productions whenever possible and with the Port Talbot Little Theatre.

In 1975–6 Comer had been Ifor, eldest son in the BBC's six-part production of *How Green Was My Valley*, adapted by the skilful Elaine Morgan from Richard Llewellyn's classic novel of 1939. It was a stellar cast with Stanley Baker (already fatally ill with cancer) as the father Gwilym Morgan and Siân Phillips as the 'Welsh Mam'.

Another Port Talbot actor was in this production: Robert Blythe. Familiar to devotees of the television comedy drama *High Hopes*, in which he plays 'Fagin', he has also done many voiceovers. Like a number of other actors from Port Talbot, he has a fine speaking voice.

Born in 1947, Blythe began his career as a surveyor. He was miserable. But a girlfriend introduced him to Briton Ferry's Little Theatre nearby. There he was given a part in the farce *Dry Rot,* acting in what had been an old 'Kinema'. Over the next few years he also performed in plays in Taibach and, as he puts it, 'I just got bitten really'. Leo Lloyd, who had carefully noted

the young actor, encouraged him but it was the teacher and aspirant actor Dennis Burgess who really made the difference: 'He was my main source of inspiration.' Blythe did his first *Under Milk Wood* with him for the Port Talbot Little Theatre. After long conversations at Burgess' home Blythe was encouraged to give up his well-paid job and go to drama school (Arts Educational in London) aged twenty-four. He has never looked back, acting across the world in more than a hundred professional plays. As with Hopkins, it was amateur dramatics and local encouragement that made the difference.

Blythe was also well aware of the Burton legacy and it meant a lot to him. His parents had taken him as a child to see him in *The Robe* and he was conscious that the whole town was talking about the man now known as Richard Burton. And Blythe grew up just two doors away from the Hopkins' bakery and home in Tanygroes Street, though with Hopkins a decade older, their paths didn't actually cross until much later in life.

Another actor Blythe has worked with is Philip Bond of Abergwynfi. The family of Bond's mother Blodwen John had settled there in the 1880s after leaving Cardiganshire. Although he spent many years based in London working on stage and making numerous television appearances – Bond is best known as Albert Frazer in twenty-four episodes of *The Onedin Line* – he returned to the Afan Valley in the late seventies. Like Blythe, his daughters are actresses (Abigail and Samantha Bond, the latter a former Miss Moneypenny in James Bond films whose television work includes *Downton Abbey, Outnumbered* and *Home Fires*).

Blythe has also acted in radio plays with Siân Owen. She represents another strand of the town's acting output, since much of her work has been in Welsh. Although many natives of Port Talbot since the inter-war years have not been Welsh speakers – a trend enhanced by incomers to Sandfields in mid-century – once the coastal strip is left behind, first language

Welsh speakers increase considerably and Welsh is predominant in Cwmafan and Pontrhydyfen.

Siân Owen grew up in Pontrhydyfen. Her mother was Richard Burton's sister, Hilda Owen. Richard Burton may not have come from a family of professional actors but his daughter, niece and great-nephew made up for this. Owen's desire to go on the stage emanated not so much from the individual example or encouragement of her famous Uncle Rich (who preferred to let her stand on her own two feet and earn her right as an actor) as from her own extrovert personality and the musical and performance talents of the Jenkins family more generally, and her mother in particular. The family boasted consummate entertainers, from Verdun, the life and soul of any party, to Graham and his solos.

The Jenkins sisters too had fine voices and sang at Eisteddfodau. Hilda was a penillion[252] singer. Siân Owen, the youngest of four children, inherited her mother's love of performance and 'I mean I just loved a stage... performance was built into me'. She participated in her first local Eisteddfod at the age of four. She took part in chapel activities and at the Urdd at local, county and national level, winning her first penillion prize at the age of nine. In 1966 the National Eisteddfod (which had first come to Port Talbot in 1932) was held in Margam and she was involved in a dramatic interpretation of *Dido and Aeneas*.

Further west in Alltwen in the Swansea Valley (now in the County Borough of Neath Port Talbot), another Siân had also begun performing aged four and loved every moment of it. Siân Phillips has recalled in her autobiography being lifted on to the Big Seat (Sedd Fawr): 'What I recited I don't remember, only that I felt happy and at home, as though I'd done this lots of times before'.[253]

Siân Owen attended the Welsh school in Pontrhydyfen – her mother had been one of those who had campaigned to get it

established – but since there was as yet no Welsh-language secondary school,[254] she went to Glan Afan. So busy was she with Eisteddfodau that only in her final year did she take part in the school play. Although she was now keen to study drama, her parents had a more secure job in mind: her sister had become a teacher. So she trained as a cardiographer at University College Hospital, London. At the same time she took private tuition at RADA in order to prepare for drama college auditions. After a year her mother relented and Owen followed in Anthony Hopkins' footsteps, going to Cardiff to follow a two-year course in drama.

This was the late sixties and there was no Welsh-language drama in the college. However, Owen played the lead in her year's final production and was immediately asked to do three television plays in Welsh for the BBC. She did film and television work in the 1970s. On one occasion, knowing that her daughter was about to appear nude in a television play (at a time when it was not possible to record programmes), Hilda Owen hastily organised a charity coffee evening to ensure that all her friends were far from their television sets.

The development of the Welsh-language soap opera *Pobol y Cwm* ('People of the Valley') from 1974, now the BBC's longest running soap opera, and the establishment of the Welsh fourth channel (S4C) from 1982 opened up opportunities for Welsh-speaking actors. Spotted by John Hefin, Owen was Agnes Spotelli in *Pobl y Cwm* for six years. A seven-year stint in *Dinas* followed and a further seven years on *Eileen*, a Radio Cymru spin-off from *Pobl y Cwm*.

The musical tradition that surrounded Siân Owen included opera. Pontrhydyfen used to have its own small operatic society and was the home not only of Richard Burton but also of the baritone Ivor Emmanuel and, more recently, the internationally renowned opera soprano Rebecca Evans.[255]

The wonderfully named Aurelia Vowles John, granddaughter

of Charles Vowles who had conducted Gilbert and Sullivan productions, had been born in 1898. She was, for more than half a century, the leading light in Port Talbot's musical performances. A pre-war accompanist, she helped to build up operettas, aided by a valuable nucleus from Pontrhydyfen. From 1947 until 1979 she was musical director of the Port Talbot and District Amateur Operatic Society, whose mission is to educate the public in both the dramatic and operatic arts. It has produced singers like Betty Brooks Richards of Margam who, from the 1950s, was the leading lady in the shows. The Society has also been a stepping-stone for professional performers. Ivor Emmanuel was the lead male singer in the reconstituted society's first show, *The Pirates of Penzance*, in 1947.[256]

The choral tradition has been strong too. The town, churches and occupational groups have formed numerous choirs, from the Afan Ladies' Choir to the Port Talbot and District Railwaymen's Choir. One of my relatives, Hubert John, was a member of the Cymric Glee and has recalled them entertaining the American tycoon Randolph Hurst and actress Marion Davies with Welsh songs at St Donat's Castle in the Vale of Glamorgan in 1936.

More recently native musical talent has been displayed through opera conductor Gareth Jones (ex-Glan Afan) who collaborates with Bryn Terfel in opera galas and Jae Alexander (née John Dummer). Jae Alexander's father was a first cousin of Dillwyn Dummer, (childhood friend of Richard Burton's) and was Burton's second cousin once removed.[257] Alexander attended St Joseph's Comprehensive and WGYTC before becoming a highly regarded West End director in musical theatre. In 2012 he conducted the Queen's Diamond Jubilee Gala at the Albert Hall.

Not surprisingly, some of the town's actors have focused on musicals. This is the route taken by Dyffryn's Daniel Graham (Williams). At Sandfields the annual show involves up to a

hundred pupils on and off stage. Former Sandfields pupils who have performed in musical theatre include Christina Modestou, a Welsh-Greek Cypriot actor and Marc Antolin, whose work ranges from the original RSC production of *Matilda* to Kafka's *The Trial* at the Young Vic. Gareth Snook's acting career has included leads in a number of West End musicals (for example, André in *Phantom of the Opera*) and he created the role of Artie Green in *Sunset Boulevard*.

Other aspects of theatre work have proved attractive too. For example, Gemma Thomas went from Sandfields to RADA and was part of the stage management team that put on the much-lauded opening and closing ceremonies at the Olympic Games in London. Some have moved from acting into tutoring, directing and writing plays. Margam's Michael Waters is involved in all three and has been the artistic director at Antic Theatre, Swansea for over a decade. He also works at RWCMD, his old college.

Taking a rather different path from fellow Port Talbot actors, John-Paul Macleod was a pupil at the Sylvia Young Drama School in London. He got his first break in films aged thirteen, starring in *The Testimony of Taliesin Jones* (2000) as a lonely boy on a Welsh farm who is drawn to faith healers.[258] He also played Helen Mirren's son in *Calendar Girls* (2003). The Glan Afan schoolboy Daniel Gammond landed a part aged fourteen in the TV series *Stella* (written by and starring Ruth Jones). He is still Little Alan four years on. He attributes his break to the support he received from the Port Talbot Amateurs (the Youth Theatre section of Port Talbot and District Amateur Operatic Society), a local authority venture run weekly from Taibach Library. It puts on an annual show and was the brainchild of Meyrick Sheen, who was its administrator for some years. It was a vital spur too for Luke Joyce, who at sixteen abandoned an engineering apprenticeship to study drama. It currently has fifty members and a waiting list.

Most of today's trained actors from Port Talbot have,

however, come under the influence of the visionary Godfrey Evans, either directly through studying at WGYTC or indirectly by being taught by those trained by Evans. The first intake at WGYTC in the mid-70s brought together Port Talbot actors who have really made their mark on Welsh theatre and television. Di Botcher was one of them. Her older brother, Stephen Botcher who died of cancer tragically young, initially stimulated her interest in drama when she saw how well regarded he was after taking the lead in the school play at Dyffryn. He went on to study drama in Cardiff and became an actor. In 1985 brother and sister acted in the same production of *The Winter's Tale* at Cardiff's recently re-opened Sherman Theatre.

Di Botcher had acted in this play at West Glamorgan where it was the founding students' first production. She had followed Stephen's example at school, though the teenager was initially unsure whether she really wanted to be cast as Mad Margaret in Gilbert and Sullivan's *Ruddigore*. But she loved being on stage and was soon following Godfrey Evans' drama pyramid by attending evening classes at the drama centre at Cwrt Sart (see Chapter 3) and WGYTC. English and Theatre Studies at Warwick followed – a route that Michael Sheen had contemplated – and postgraduate work at London's Webber Douglas then repertory across Britain. Working in England with seven years at the National Theatre and West End musicals (including *Chicago*) eventually saw her return to a focus on Wales and she now divides her time between London and Port Talbot.

Di Botcher played Nanny West in *Downton Abbey* and has appeared in dramas such as *Bleak House* and *Sherlock*. She is best known in Wales for her characters in television soaps such as *Belonging* and *Stella*. When she played the lead in a 2006 revival at Cardiff's New Theatre of *A Kiss on the Bottom* by the comic playwright Frank Vickery, her performance in this tale of mature women on a cancer ward was compared to 'a gorgeous Gucci dress that stands out from the crowd, subtly accessorised

by her talented co-stars'.[259] One co-star was Margam's Jennifer Hill who had acted in many television dramas as well as appearing in the 1982 film *Giro City* (as did the ubiquitous Robert Blythe).

That first WGYTC production, *The Winter's Tale*, had Kevin Allen (from Loughor) as Florizel. When he came to write and direct the dark comedy film *Twin Town* set in Swansea and Port Talbot he cast Di Botcher as Rhys Ifans's mother. In 2014 Allen and Ifans worked together on new film versions of *Dan y Wenallt/Under Milk Wood* shot in Solva, Pembrokeshire. Having played Mrs Dai Bread One that year, she now became Mrs Dai Bread Two in Welsh and English.

Francine Morgan was another member of that first cohort at WGYTC, and played Hermione in *The Winter's Tale*. She describes Godfrey Evans' impact as 'incalculable'. Going to WGYTC widened horizons, introducing students to young people from different areas and backgrounds. The residential courses prepared students for intensive work in the future. And as Kevin Matherick, head of drama at Sandfields from 1980–92 explains, it meant that the staff's skills were constantly evolving too: it generated 'massive staff development'.

Although Richard Burton and Anthony Hopkins have clearly been inspirational, for many of today's actors their role models have come from those within their own community who broke through barriers, along with their drama teachers and Godfrey Evans himself. Gary Williams (now known as Gary Lagden) encapsulates this viewpoint. Born in 1972, he saw a production of *Charlie and the Chocolate Factory* at Sandfields Comprehensive at the age of ten. Acting in it was a young actor called Darren Lawrence who had gone to WGYTC and then trained at Central before becoming a successful actor and director.[260] Lagden explains that he was 'the first person I had heard of from Sandfields to go to drama school in London... This had a big effect on me. The idea that it was possible to be an actor'.

Gary Lagden's drama teacher was Kevin Matherick. Lagden calls him 'a force of nature, he was absolutely committed to creating an environment that encouraged excellence'. As for Godfrey Evans, he 'saw in young people the essence of creativity'. Admittedly, Lagden is looking back on all this thirty years after he started at Sandfields. But although his appreciation is couched in more sophisticated language than he is likely to have deployed at the time, there is plenty of evidence to suggest that he and many others understood how fortunate they were from the start.

Lagden went to RADA after WGYTC, a move made possible by receiving a full grant from West Glamorgan County Council. This factor distinguishes aspiring working-class actors of his era from today's hopefuls who face markedly different economic opportunities and educational policies with their attendant 'calcification of social mobility'.[261]

Remarkably for his profession, Lagden has never been out of work. He made a strategic move, opting to work with young people. The late Noël Greig wrote a number of one-man shows especially for him. Greig's three stories for Lagden and the East Midlands Company Tangere Arts were extended poetic versions of classic fairy tales. Lagden has toured with them from Derbyshire to Denmark, Russia as well as Wales. His recent work has been at London's Unicorn Theatre. He has also directed Othello at RADA as part of their Shakespeare in Schools Project. And completing that circle, he and Sandfields' Darren Lawrence have worked together at Manchester's Royal Exchange Theatre on a version of *The Rime of the Ancient Mariner.*

As the Appendix shows, a younger generation of actors from Sandfields has continued the tradition. Matthew Aubrey is one. Born in 1988, his father had been taught at Sandfields by Godfrey Evans. Helen John was Aubrey's teacher. She had been a pupil herself at Sandfields in the early 1980s, where Kevin Matherick taught her. Aubrey and his dad used to watch old

westerns and war films together then go chasing imaginary soldiers up Margam Mountain and, as he now realises, acting even though they weren't aware of it at the time. He had never seen a theatre but he took the Great Hall for granted.

On leaving school he followed his father into the Works but, partly due to his mother stressing the value of Gorseinon College, he did the BTEC there, finding it transformative. Teaching there were former WGYTC students Vivienne Buckley, currently WGYTC's Artistic Director and Nick Evans, now Associate Director of WGYTC and acclaimed musical director (his West End hits include *Jesus Christ Superstar* and *Billy Elliot The Musical*). Two-thirds of Aubrey's fellow students in the acting strand alone (not counting musical theatre) went on to drama school.

Aubrey won a place at the RWCMD in Cardiff. He left early for a part in *Framed*, a TV film about the wartime removal of the art treasures of London's National Gallery to north Wales. A small role in the film *Made in Dagenham* followed, then a six-week BBC drama in Cape Town playing the part of a soldier in the Alan Bleasdale drama, *The Sinking of the Laconia*. It was not the first or last time that Aubrey would play the part of a soldier. He attributes this to his accent and. the fact that he is skinny and working class.

On his return Aubrey began auditions for the lead role of Albert Narracott in the National's immensely popular dramatisation of Michael Morpurgo's *War Horse*. In April 2010 he became the third Albert to be cast and played this part for a year. He did eight three-hour shows a week. One of the youngest in the cast, he found it immensely helpful and 'almost like an extra year of college'. Aubrey has also done a season with the RSC at Stratford. He had a lead in Brecht's *A Life of Galileo*, and he has been an acclaimed Mr Collins in *Pride and Prejudice* at Sheffield's Crucible Theatre.

In 2012 Aubrey was one of the cast of six in the drama about the twenty-four year-old US soldier accused of releasing 250,00

pieces of classified information about military operations in the Iraq and Afghan conflicts and sentenced to three years in prison. *The Radicalisation of Bradley Manning* was part of the second season of original, experimental productions from National Theatre Wales (NTW). It opened at the Tasker Milward School, Haverfordwest where the teenage Bradley Manning had been a pupil for a couple of years. The soldier's mother was in the audience on the first night and Aubrey (the same age as Manning) told me that this was the best night of his life. Close on 9,000 people in seventy-six countries watched a live streaming of the play. John E. McGrath's award-winning production was at the Edinburgh Fringe the following year.

Aubrey's school friend Kyle Rees was also in the play. Rees studied at the Royal Scottish Academy of Music and Drama after Gorseinon and his credits include a part in *Pride*, the BAFTA-winning film (based on a true story) about the alliance between striking miners and their families in south-west Wales in 1984–5 and gay and lesbian activists from London. He has one of the lead parts in the new major TV series for the US and UK, *The Bastard Executioner*, about a medieval warrior knight. It is being filmed in south Wales and also stars Matthew Rhys.

For today's Port Talbot actors, Michael Sheen is their local hero. 'I grew up adoring him; he's such an amazing actor,' Aubrey explains.[262] Part of the admiration stems from the fact that 'He's the most normal film star'. Aubrey and fellow former Sandfields pupils Kyle Rees, Darren Lawrence, Francine Morgan and Jordan Bernarde (who studied at RWCMD) have a further reason to appreciate and be proud of Sheen. For, thanks to him, they participated in a huge tribute to their hometown, the staging of *The Passion* in 2011 and the subsequent film *The Gospel of Us*.

5

Remembering the town

Rob Brydon has frequently referenced Port Talbot in his
television work, whether as the punch line for a joke in the
comedy panel game *Would I Lie to You?* or in the repartee of his
one-man stage shows. His television chat show in 2010
displayed the steelworks as a backdrop. He even smuggled in a
mention when interviewing Neil Diamond in Brooklyn for ITV's
Neil Diamond: One Night Only.[263] Much of Brydon's work
revolves around issues of identity and loyalty and the Port
Talbot tag has served him well, providing the opportunity for a
quick laugh apparently at the expense of its inhabitants but
always delivered knowingly so that this audience is also aware
of the pull of the place. He admits that as he has matured, so a
greater awareness has developed of how much a place shapes a
person.

But how has support for the town been reflected in the
actions of its other big stars? Michael Sheen's sustained
relationship with Port Talbot has earned him plaudits but there
is continuing debate about Richard Burton and Anthony
Hopkins' involvement with their hometown. Yet this needs to
be understood in context. When both Burton and Hopkins were
growing up the silver screen and America in particular had an
irresistible appeal. Wales did not seem fashionable. The Welsh
language was not favoured even within its own land. A
distinctive Welsh theatre had not emerged let alone a Welsh
television channel and film industry with its BAFTA Cymru

Awards. The star Richard Burton may have become a friend of Lord Harlech's and involved in the start of HTV but television broadcasting didn't even begin within Wales until 1952, and although the numbers watching it grew very rapidly, half of Welsh households still had no television at the end of the fifties.[264] Burton and Hopkins inevitably rode away into the sunset. There would be much heralded returns for the occasional twenty-four hours – the magic carpet in reverse – but they could not stay. Neither superstar could really go back once they belonged to a wider world.

And despite some ambivalent attitudes about Wales and their home turf bound up with fluctuating senses of personal worth, Burton and Hopkins have both made a significant contribution to their erstwhile communities. This has been expressed through the considerable achievement of putting their town on the international map. It has also manifested itself in other ways and this chapter examines how these two stars have reconciled Hollywood and 'home'.

There is no doubting Richard Burton's pride in Wales. Just before the Investiture of the Prince of Wales, a time of heightened militant nationalism, he distanced himself from violence and Home Rule but affirmed an irrefragable belief in the importance of the Welsh language.[265] He once told me that, being Welsh, I was a member of the most exclusive club in the world. But what Wales – and in this context what Port Talbot – are we talking about?

Drawing primarily upon the actor's diaries, the historian Chris Williams has argued convincingly that Burton's relationship with Wales reflects a duality between on the one hand a public spirited defence of his homeland that displayed the stock tropes of patriotism and, on the other hand, a private longing for a world he had lost and which, though preserved in aspic in his powerful memory, no longer existed.[266]

Williams does not fall into the trap of making Burton's Welsh

acting roles necessarily synonymous with his beliefs or symptomatic of his commitment to Wales. He focuses rather on his daily life, suggesting that he was 'a quintessential *performer* of Wales and Welshness'[267] and he notes that, despite all his public declarations of being Welsh, Burton's private diaries lack such attention. Burton's public pronouncements were defined in opposition. They suggest most about how he did *not* wish to be perceived. Despite his lifestyle and those who surrounded him, he could not see himself as anything but a product of the working class and he never wanted to be presumed to be part of the English establishment. Williams also suggests that, although a patriot, Burton was not a nationalist. He was certainly impatient of political nationalism but he did like to see himself as a cultural nationalist, steeped in his nation's literature and culture.

In many ways Burton experienced in an extreme form the classic dilemma of the exile: unable to return to where he had come from but never fully fitting in anywhere else. The south Walian novelist Menna Gallie, born in the Swansea Valley just five years before Burton, spent most of her adult life outside Wales. She became increasingly wary of romanticising what she called 'the long hiraethus [268] years' of living outside Wales:[269]

> How is one in love with the valleys to pull out the shrinking weeds of sentimentality? How is one to reject the blandishments of distorted memory? And how is one to accept the realities of the valleys as they are today?

She recognised that harking back to the inter-war years not only distorted the experience of a time of hardship but also had implications for the present. She suggested that: 'If we persist in seeing Wales, and more especially the valleys, in this old-fashioned light we are committing ourselves to, imprisoning ourselves in, what has become only History.'

In a sense Menna Gallie was voicing what Richard Burton could not fully recognise or perhaps face: the fact that his point of reference was a Pontrhydyfen and a Port Talbot that now only existed in the imagination. But this was, of course, hardly surprising since he had travelled so far in literal and symbolic terms from his roots.

The pressures and loneliness of international stardom magnified this dislocation and Burton's status as a tax exile prevented him from owning property in the UK. His fame meant that he seemed to inhabit a liminal world outside 'ordinary' society and this could render him a virtual prisoner. I remember an evening when Elizabeth Taylor's teenage daughter Liza was on her way home from boarding school to the private suite high up in the Dorchester Hotel (beyond the reach of the guests' lifts) where the Burtons used to stay. Then came a kidnap threat. It came to nothing and was carefully kept from the media but what struck me was not only the stress it inevitably generated but also the fact that such terrifying scenarios were not that unusual.

An assessment of what Richard Burton did for Port Talbot needs first to recognise the disjuncture between his undoubted celebration of where he came from (and even that wasn't straightforward, since he could lay claim to both Pontrhydyfen and Taibach) and his ability to be anything more than tangentially involved in the life of the town in the second half of the twentieth century. Having said this, there were, nevertheless, a number of ways in which he provided vital support and generated pride.

The first was in his continued involvement over the years with his family and local causes. For example, the latter was shown in his financial support for the Invalid Tricycle Association locally (Burton was president and my father a vice-president). And in the 1970s the Burtons presented a cup for a male voice choir's competition to the annual South Wales

Miners' Eisteddfod in Porthcawl. He also sponsored the memorial (in the South Wales Miners' Library) to the Welsh International Brigade members who died in the Spanish Civil War.

Although a number of his siblings and their families moved away, Burton's eldest brother Tom, along with Verdun, Hilda and Graham[270] remained in the area and David was nearby in Swansea. Burton was generous to them all, buying houses, providing cheques twice a year and sending lavish gifts from America. Over the years letters from Cis and the others poured out gratitude for their brother's largesse.[271] He had numerous nieces and nephews and arranged for many relatives to go to parties at the Dorchester. For Elizabeth Taylor's fortieth birthday celebrations in February 1972 a telegram invited the Jenkins siblings and spouses to the lavish event at Budapest's Duna Inter-Continental Hotel stressing: 'ALL EXPENSES PAID INCLUDING CAVIAR AND BLOATERS'.[272]

Members of Burton's family would visit him in London, Switzerland and the United States as well as on location. When Graham Jenkins was in the audience of *Camelot* on Broadway in 1960, he heard his brother ad-lib as King Arthur and create an extra knight, declaring 'Arise, Sir Graham of Afan'.[273] Although Burton had grown up in Taibach, Pontrhydyfen in the Afan Valley became his focal point as a film star, not least because this was where sister Hilda lived. After Cis moved to England, it was to Hilda's home that the actor would gravitate. So a Rolls Royce could sometimes be seen in Pontrhydyfen.[274]

From the start the press reported in detail on the progress of their local boy made good. Visits home were proudly charted. In January 1955 readers of the *Glamorgan Gazette* were told that Richard Burton had come home to Caradoc Street for Christmas.[275] He had been making *Prince of Players* and 'one of Aberavon's most arduous supporters' attended the annual fixtures, the rugby match against Maesteg on Christmas Day

115

and the Boxing Day battle with Neath. His next task was filming in Spain and Greece for *Alexander the Great*. Brother Ivor and his wife Gwen were to accompany him from Cwmafan (Ivor had been a collier and was a bricklayer after being invalided out of the army). He began working for Burton as his right-hand man. It was reported that niece Marian from Caradoc Street would go with them and do a film test.[276] She did, thanks to Richard Burton, secure work in the industry (though not as actor). Graham Jenkins would later double for his brother in the films of *The VIPS* and *Becket*.

It was on this 1955 visit that Burton handed his wife Sybil a red ribbon. As she unwound it, she discovered that it led to a convertible red sports car awaiting her in the street. I remember as a child being told the story of this extraordinary Christmas gift. Richard Burton had married Sybil Williams in 1949. She was from Tylorstown in the Rhondda. Her parents had died when she was in her teens and she too had lived for a time with an older married sister. She trained at LAMDA and had a bit part in *The Last Days of Dolwyn* where she met Richard Burton. 'Syb', as he called her, was a great hit with the family.

A few days later it was reported that Burton and his brothers had attended the annual Christmas party of the Treherbert Police Sub-division where brother David was stationed. The following January the film star accepted the presidency of the Aberavon Motor Cycle and Light Car Club.[277] But increasingly, and especially after the filming of *Cleopatra* in 1961–2, the relationship to the town was and had to be different.

Into a Britain in which there was no Internet or mobile phones or even much central heating, came news of 'Le Scandale' in Rome and all that ensued. The exoticism of the story still fascinates.[278] The Burtons became legendary. One book about them is subtitled *The Marriage of the Century*.[279] Despite the decent wages in the steelworks in the Port Talbot of the 1960s, many homes did not even have telephones. In a

place that didn't see the large-scale trappings of wealth and status, the Burtons were unofficial royalty.

Prefiguring the modern preoccupation with celebrity culture, the pre-eminent position that the Burton-Taylor marriage guaranteed across the world spelt some reflected glory, for it gave Port Talbot fame. There remained something of a proprietorial interest in the activities of this home-grown superstar, quite apart from the fascination with Elizabeth Taylor.

The fact that the height of Burton's fame and films coincided with the town's most affluent times softened open criticism of impossibly lavish lifestyles and marital breakdown, though those who knew Sybil appreciated her qualities and were loyal to the first Mrs Burton, who was also the mother of their two children, Kate and Jessica.

Richard Burton's evident generosity to his extended family, and the fact that many still remembered him as first a schoolboy then as a remarkably fine British-based stage actor, helped to disguise the fact that the days when he could watch Aberavon play or drink in the Miner's Arms without a media frenzy were no more. A letter from the warden of the Taibach Youth Centre in March 1962 says he would like to see Burton next week 'but Rome is an age away'.[280]

If Burton's image of Wales and Port Talbot in particular was like a frozen snapshot, then so too were popular perceptions of the town's hero rooted in a fondly imagined past. He might still make it to Cardiff Arms Park for the occasional rugby international but by the mid-sixties attendance at all public events had to be carefully choreographed. In the early seventies the Burtons were unable even to dine in the rarefied atmosphere of the Dorchester Hotel without attracting undue attention. Meals there were confined to their suite.

Burton helped out others besides his family. When Elizabeth Taylor's sons Michael and Christopher Wilding were at Millfield School in Somerset, in line with the ethos of the school, he paid

annually for scholarships to enable Welsh boys to become pupils there. But most relevant is the way that he advanced the careers of local actors. His address book, dating from 1948 included, amongst contact details for the leading actors in the English-speaking world, Port Talbot's performers Dennis Burgess, Doug Blackwell, Catherine Dolan, Brinley Jenkins, Ray Pike, Dai 'Dwsh' and Ivor Emmanuel.[281]

Ivor Lewis Emmanuel, whose family had been virtually obliterated by a wartime bomb, was one of those who benefitted. He was just two years younger than Burton. A sign on entering Pontrhydyfen declares it to be the birthplace of Richard Burton, Ivor Emmanuel and Rebecca Evans. In fact Emmanuel had been born in Margam. However, by the time he started school, he was living in Pontrhydyfen. He began singing young. He was in Port Talbot's Snowflakes choir on the eve of the war and participated in opera and drama in Pontrhydyfen, as well as in the Port Talbot Operatic Society. From the age of fourteen he worked, first as a miner then as an engineering apprentice in the steelworks. His ambition, however, was to sing on the professional stage. It was said that he used to carry a wind-up gramophone to a spot in the Afan Valley where he would listen to recordings of Caruso.

In the summer of 1948 he was unsuccessful in an audition for D'Oyly Carte and soon after this it seems that he met Richard Burton in a pub in London. The actor pulled strings and a telegram arrived as Emmanuel was on his afternoon shift, instructing him to audition the next day at the Theatre Royal Drury Lane for the Rodgers and Hammerstein musical *Oklahoma!* This record-breaking show starred Howard Keel. It gave a vital kick-start to a glittering career for this 'handsome, strapping figure' with 'virile looks' and a 'muscular voice'.[282] Emmanuel was in the musical for nine months. He joined D'Oyly Carte in 1950 and did a six-month US tour with the company.

He also appeared in West End musicals such as *South Pacific*. He finally secured a lead role in a musical in 1957 in *Damn Yankee* but it was television that made him. Between 1958 and 1964 he was the lead singer on a Sunday evening television show made by TWW (Television Wales and the West) called *Gwlad y Gân* ('Land of Song'). Once a month about ten million people across the UK would watch and listen to Ivor Emmanuel and the Pontcanna Children's Choir singing in the Welsh language in the first bilingual musical show networked from Wales. When he died the *Stage* described him as 'one of Britain's most popular singing stars of the fifties and sixties'.[283] In 1960 he sang in the first televised edition of the Royal Variety Performance.

Yet Ivor Emmanuel is chiefly remembered for a different reason. In 1964 he was Private Owen in the epic film *Zulu*, starring and produced by Richard Burton's friend Stanley Baker.[284] This dramatisation of the 1879 battle for Rorke's Drift in South Africa's Natal province famously intensified the Welsh contribution to the event and had Emmanuel's character leading the soldiers into battle with an unforgettable rendition of *Men of Harlech*.[285] The singing was recorded on a hillside near Baker's native Ferndale with Emmanuel and members of the local male voice choir. The film's use of Technirama photography aided box office success and enduring popularity. Burton provided the narration.

Emmanuel's later years were not in the limelight. A musical version of *How Green Was My Valley* on Broadway (entitled *A Time for Singing*) flopped in 1966. He spent his last twenty-five years on the Costa del Sol and lost his life savings when a Spanish bank collapsed. He died in his eightieth year in 2007. His glittering mid-century career had been made possible by a combination of his powerful baritone voice, the operatic culture of his local community and the support of Richard Burton.

Burton also created opportunities for another ambitious man from Port Talbot. Dennis Burgess, who had been at the Sec with

him, was one more boy who was under the spell of Philip Burton's teaching. He was in *Gallows Glorious*. He became a primary school teacher then taught drama at Glan Afan. But he remained committed to the stage. One of his former pupils at Groes School has recalled how he would take the children up the nearby Brombil Valley and encourage them to imagine that ferns were spears that they could use for dramatic chases. He acted with the YMCA Players and the Wayfarers and directed for the Little Theatre where his wife Glenys did the costumes.

In 1955, just as Anthony Hopkins was finding his feet, the *Gazette* commented on Burgess' 'remarkable talent, his authority and his amazing range'. Especially praised was his command of the spoken language. These qualities, it suggested, were 'very seldom equalled in the amateur field'.[286] Five years later, his 'casual, irascible stage style' was thought to suit perfectly his role as Elyot Chase in Noel Coward's *Private Lives* for the Little Theatre.[287]

Burgess was still teaching aged forty. He and Glenys were looking after his invalid mother at their home in Pentyla, Port Talbot but he remained anxious for more than 'the amateur field'. His break was due to Burton. The two men had remained in touch. Burton told Burgess in 1967 that he adored his friend's mother and would never forget her kindness to him when he was a schoolboy. His letters to Burgess were informal, frank, fond and signed: 'Much love to you both from us both, Rich'.[288]

That October Burton wrote from his yacht *Kalizma* in Sardinia inviting Burgess to the opening night of the film of *Dr Faustus*. He suggested that they collect the couple in Cardiff in their new jet plane and bring them to Rome. In the same letter Burton told him:

> I think, and so does E, that we can get you out of your present rat-race and into ours but it will take some time.[289]

He added that it might take up to a year to achieve and suggested that they move to the Cardiff or Bristol area.

Mrs Burgess's ill-health, however, militated against a move and career change. Burgess continued acting locally: his performance in the Little Theatre's *Tartuffe* in 1968 was described as 'awe-inspiring'. His mother died in 1970 and after this he took the plunge. He got work with the Welsh Theatre Company in Cardiff. In March 1972 Burton wrote that: 'We are both delighted that you finally made the break with the monotony of multiplication tables and broke for free country'.[290] He was in Hungary filming *Bluebeard*. He arranged with the film's director Edward Dmytryk for Burgess to have one day's filming. There were two small parts going. Burton reckoned that the role of a coroner with about ten lines was the one less likely to end up on the cutting room floor and it included a close up.

He sent a telegram to Burgess asking him to fly to Budapest in a few weeks' time. Burton would pay all expenses. Burgess could now get his foot in the 'Film Door'.[291] Burton was keen for Glenys to come too. The telegram instructed him to bring a dark suit, white shirt and sober tie and 'your talent'. Burton followed this with a long letter. Conscious that embarking on a career in films in middle age was far from the usual route to success, he joked that Elizabeth Taylor, who was, he stressed, invariably right, believed that he would 'make it'. She saw him as the exception that would prove the rule.

Well aware that this film was hardly the sort of work that he was worthy of, Burton attempted, not very convincingly, to justify his abysmal choice by claiming that it was due to his children's wish for him to do a horror film. He told Burgess that what mattered was that his friend could be listed in Spotlight (the UK's premier casting agency) in a film starring Richard Burton and Raquel Welch. By then he reckoned they would have found an agent. He stressed – sounding as though he needed to

persuade himself – that, despite being comic-horror, it was still a major film. He suggested that Burgess cast his eye over other scripts he was currently considering so that they could 'see what we can cull'.[292]

Warming to his advisory role, Burton added that Burgess needed to put together a list of parts he had played. He suggested he omit the fact that they had been in amateur productions. Many years ago he had helped to make up a curriculum vitae for the Welsh actor Hugh Griffith who was also entering the business late. They quoted notices from critics long dead and for performances he had never given but it had secured him a season at Stratford and there had been no looking back.

Burton's advice was revealing. Philip Burton's erstwhile pupil was adamant that under no circumstances should Burgess act with a Welsh accent and suggested instead a middle European voice like the one he was adopting. The tone and length of Burton's letter suggests that he enjoyed playing the role of tutor. He advised Burgess to ignore stage directions since directors tended not to keep to them 'and I will be over his [Dmytryk's] shoulder'.[293] It was worth learning his lines rather than reading them and useful to fiddle with props like a pince-nez.

Burgess duly did his bit and Burton wrote to tell him how 'delighted' he, Elizabeth and the director were with his work. It was 'Marvellous for a first time in camera and a close up with no rehearsals'.[294]

But on 28 April Burton told his friend, 'I have been through a great deal since I saw you last'.[295] His world had just fallen apart with the death of his beloved brother Ivor, who had been a paraplegic since a terrible accident four years earlier at *Pays de Galles,* the Burtons' Swiss home. Although Burton had assured Burgess the previous month that he had been 'stone-cold sober' for almost two years, 'apart from periodic explosions',[296] the death of the brother who had for many years

been like a father to him, hastened the return of frequent 'explosions' and, it would seem, the end of a decade of being faithful to Elizabeth Taylor. The couple would soon separate for the first time.

Burton did not, however, forget Dennis Burgess. In October 1972 a telegram arrived in Port Talbot announcing that he had secured a part for him in *Death in Rome* based on a novel of the same name.[297] It drew on a true war story about the mass shootings of Italians in Rome in a German reprisal after Italian partisans had killed one tenth of their number of SS troops in 1944. The film was renamed *Massacre in Rome*. Produced by Carlo Ponti, it starred Burton and Marcello Mastroianni. Burgess played an SS officer under Burton's command.[298]

Dennis Burgess never became very well known but he made a decent living as an actor. During the second half of the 1970s he and Glenys left Port Talbot and moved to Chesham in Buckinghamshire, which was handy for film studios. He appeared in a few other films including David Lynch's award-winning *The Elephant Man*, in which Anthony Hopkins had a lead role alongside an unrecognisable John Hurt.

Burgess also worked in television from 1974 onwards. In the television adaptation of G. K. Chesterton's *Father Brown* he was Hercule Flambeau (Kenneth More played Father Brown) and he was one of the stars of the ITV Cold War series *The Sandbaggers*. It was as he was driving home from an episode in this series in 1980 that he had a heart attack. He died before the end of the year, aged just fifty-four, yet another Port Talbot actor who never reached the age of sixty.

Richard Burton has not been alone in drawing frequent attention to his hometown. Anthony Hopkins also carries it with him even though he too has moved far away. His relationship to the place has, however, been somewhat different and, at times, quite ambivalent, as well as seeking to avoid that revealing term the 'Stage Welshman'. Hopkins does not speak

Welsh and has never been a rugby follower.[299] In contrast to Burton whose family remained in the town, Hopkins was an only child and his parents moved to Laleston near Bridgend then to Caerleon where they ran a pub before retirement. Hopkins has had less reason than Burton to return to Port Talbot.

He has nevertheless remained in touch with old family friends. To celebrate his seventieth birthday he held a lavish party at the Orangery in Margam Park on Christmas Eve 2007. It was reputed to have cost £200,000. The venue was transformed with new curtains, carpet and furniture. There was a male voice choir. Two hundred guests were invited including the current owners of Hopkins' former Margam home and some of the old YMCA actors.

Hopkins' generosity has helped drama students. When the young Matthew Rhys wanted to study at RADA he wrote to the actor and was offered £3,000.[300] The Anthony Hopkins Charitable Foundation has helped students to study at the RWCMD. In 1988 he gave £300,000 towards renovation costs. The £22.5 million renovation programme was completed in 2011. The RWCMD is also the National Conservatoire of Wales and Cardiff Castle's former stables and courtyard have been converted into practice rooms and a recording studio. There are also three performance spaces. Hopkins is acknowledged as their best-known alumnus and the award-winning Anthony Hopkins Centre is testimony to how he is regarded.

The beautifully designed, purpose-built campus in the grounds of Cardiff Castle also pays tribute to Burton with its 160-seat Richard Burton Theatre. At a Royal Gala held at Buckingham Palace to celebrate the college's sixtieth anniversary, Dame Elizabeth Taylor presented to Prince Charles (Patron of the College) a bronze bust of her former husband. It is displayed in the foyer of the theatre.[301] Their resident company of actors is called The Richard Burton Company.

Clwyd Theatr Cymru (until 1998 known as Theatr Clwyd) in Mold, Flintshire has the Anthony Hopkins Theatre. In 1994 Hopkins had performed there in his first theatre role for five years and made his first appearance on a Welsh stage for more than thirty years in the stage play of *August*. It was a first in other ways too, marking his directorial debut.[302] Support for north Wales was also shown in Hopkins' generous £1 million donation to the Snowdonia Appeal (of which he was president) to help purchase part of the iconic mountain.

Hopkins has, over the years, responded positively to appeals made by the local community in Port Talbot about issues such as the right of way in the Brombil Valley (close to his Wern Road home) and the ongoing problems of the M4. Port Talbot's YMCA has long benefitted from Hopkins' support as its Patron and in 2008 its young members presented him with a plaque of a Welsh dragon inscribed with Albert Einstein's words about imagination being everything. He has given them encouragement, publicity, posters, photographs, his director's chair and memorabilia such as the sword of Zorro. An Anthony Hopkins Performance Academy existed for a time run by Rhys Matthews (actor and grandson of Doug Rees whom Hopkins knew in his early acting days). The YMCA has a hostel for homeless young men named The Anthony Hopkins House.

In 1994 the Borough of Port Talbot made Sir Anthony Hopkins CBE an Honorary Freeman of the County Borough of Port Talbot. In his speech he described how he used to take walks round town with his maternal grandfather, recalling former buildings such as the old market and the Walnut Tree Hotel. Six years later, in a rather different ceremony in California, attended by Steven Spielberg and John Travolta, he became a US citizen. For some this was seen as a betrayal. There were even calls for him to renounce his Freedom status. Yet Hopkins already had dual citizenship and the fact that he is so highly regarded internationally remains for many in Port

Talbot a source of intense pride rather than regret. Anyway, this step should not really have been seen as surprising. For a start Hopkins had, from his youth, embraced American culture, most notably its films. He had effectively left Wales in 1957 and had long been based in California.

The United States has been good to Hopkins. Despite his consummate theatre and film roles in the UK, he is best known for playing Hannibal Lecter in *The Silence of the Lambs*. Here was a film that, in the words of Hopkins' biographer Quentin Falk, 'didn't so much open as erupt'.[303] Although Hopkins was not the first to play that part (the Scots actor Brian Cox had done so in *Manhunter* in 1986) and he was only on screen for just over sixteen minutes, he won an Oscar for Best Actor in 1992. His award was dedicated to his mother. She spent the last few years of her life in the States living close to her son. She died in 2003. Hopkins' punishing film schedules (demanding even for somebody not in their seventies) haven't helped physical contact with south Wales.

Living in one country does not preclude an emotional attachment to another. 'I come from' has more than one meaning. A location might have been left in a physical sense but it is shorthand too for what it represents and, crucially, can suggest a pride in this place. If Richard Burton and more recently Michael Sheen and Rob Brydon are known for including a reference to Port Talbot in virtually every interview they have given, the same can probably be said for Hopkins (even though in some cases the actors have been responding to interviewers determined to press a point about their 'humble' origins and Welshness). Port Talbot is, as Di Botcher puts it, 'part of their psyche'.

In recent years, Hopkins seems to have displayed an increased identification with his hometown. He has never shied away from stressing how he suffered in school. Indeed, the language with which he has described his alienation – such as

feeling as though he were on Mars and thinking and speaking 'Martian' – has been extreme. He has not eased up on the image of the loner with the demanding father and the teachers who saw him as an unmitigated failure. But he now puts a different gloss on all this. Age, distance, a happy marriage, sobriety, faith, the reflection involved in writing of memoirs, all these factors could have affected how he now chooses to remember his past. What was once represented as somewhat negative and destructive – a sort of looking back in anger – is now seen positively as part of a learning curve, a vital contribution to making him the man he became.

It was in St Davids Cathedral in Pembrokeshire that Hopkins and his wife of ten years Stella Arroyave chose to renew their wedding vows at the end of 2012. During this trip they called in at his old home in Wern Road, Margam. Hopkins had explained the previous year that he loved to return to the scene of his childhood and that he could still hear the 'clink of the gate, the knock on the door and still smell that time'.[304]

One way in which he has recently rekindled memories of this childhood and paid homage to it has been through classical music. From an early age he had displayed musical aptitude. His mother even dreamed of her son becoming a concert pianist. Manuscript paper was purchased from Salter's Music Stores in Neath and he had begun composing young. Hopkins has remained a talented pianist and in recent years has devoted more time to composition as well as to painting landscapes in his studio. Ironically, early in his career during a season at the Phoenix Theatre, Leicester after leaving RADA, he briefly changed his name to Anthony Yeats (his mother's maiden name) lest he be confused with Antony Hopkins (1921–2014) the classical composer, conductor and radio broadcaster.

The renowned Dutch musician André Rieu has conducted (and recorded) his Johann Strauss orchestra in an arrangement of a waltz Hopkins had composed in 1964 when a young actor at

Liverpool Playhouse. Years later the actor scored it for full orchestra and attended in July 2011 the performance of 'And the Waltz Goes On' in Vienna. In that same month he joined the City of Birmingham Symphony Orchestra on stage at Birmingham's Symphony Hall for the live recording of an album of his orchestrated piano compositions and film scores. The following day the concert was reprised at St David's Hall in Cardiff.

Entitled *Composer*, the album/DVD invokes memories of Hopkins' childhood. His down to earth father had worried that his son was escaping into a dream world of music and imagination run riot. Many decades later Hopkins has recreated through his music and his descriptions of each piece, an idyll of a boy's childhood in Wales with the spotlight on Margam.

One track is simply called 'Margam'. It was not its original title. This piano music had been written by Hopkins in the mid-1990s for the film *August* and given the film's name. In the Notes accompanying the CD, Hopkins writes that the place he lived in 'was like an Eden of fields and farms, meadows of wild flowers, trees and woods'. In these recollections it is always summertime. Three tracks are entitled '1947'. This was when the family moved from Margam to Taibach.

The first of the '1947' tracks is called 'Circus' and conveys the child's thrill of having the circus in town. The young Hopkins was taken to see it for the first time in August 1947. Sitting with his grandfather in the front row, he was entranced by the elephants and 'Marion the Elephant Girl' (a more recent version of Michael Sheen's ancestor Mary Ann Blower). In contrast to the tone of the previous music, however, Notes for this track alert us to illusion. Hopkins suggests the fragility of the familiar escapist dream of the circus. Marion with her sparkles and sequins was a bleached blonde and 'sixty if she was a day'.

Another track is called 'Bracken Road'. This is the street behind Wern Road where an uncle, aunt and cousins lived. The Notes extend the romance by focusing on another, somewhat

filmic, image: that of the sound of music in the distance. Hopkins explains that one warm summer afternoon he was heading for Wern Farm and the fields when, passing the corner of Bracken Road, he caught the sound of orchestra music played on a wireless in a kitchen. The piano, the 'lush strings and a solitary trumpet' evoked 'something lost and romantic'.

The final track is 'The Plaza', in homage to the Port Talbot cinema that used to transport him to another world. This was originally entitled 'Schizoid Salsa' – he had adored Carmen Miranda 'with the big fruit salad on her head' – and was composed for a sci-fi fantasy called *Slipstream* that Hopkins had scripted and taken to the 2007 Sundance Festival.

He talked about the importance of music in his life when he was in the UK for the concert, putting forward a new explanation of his decision to go to the Welsh College of Music and Drama and emphasising the first part of its title by suggesting that he was at the time more interested in music than acting.[305] He claimed, as he has often done, that he has never felt he belongs in the acting world. Unlike Burton who, at least in part, embraced the Hollywood world, Hopkins has always been wary. Perhaps, though, a distinction should be made between the public lifestyle of the film star, which, despite opting to live in California has never been to his taste, and the craft of acting.

When he was made a Fellow of the Academy at the BAFTA awards in 2008, Hopkins chose in his acceptance speech to provide his audience with an image that he said was a metaphor for his life in films. He recalled how, as a boy starting off in the YMCA in Port Talbot:

I used to jump on the back of those double-decker buses and hold on to the white pole. I never wanted to go inside. I used to love swinging on the thing, you know, the wind in my face.[306]

It's a powerful, romantic picture that will resonate with many. And it is striking how the town has now come to connote freedom for him rather than restriction. Anthony Hopkins may have left Port Talbot but Port Talbot most certainly hasn't left him.

6

Pride and Passion

At the beginning of this century Michael Sheen was identified as one of the 'Taff Pac', part of a group of nine modern actors proud to identify themselves as Welsh. They included Jonathan Pryce, Rhys Ifans, Ioan Gruffudd and Matthew Rhys.[307] Sheen has, for thirteen years, been based in Los Angeles primarily because this is where his teenage daughter Lily lives (with her mother, Sheen's former partner Kate Beckinsale), though America is also the source of much of his work and social life. Yet, remarkably, he still spends a considerable amount time in Wales as well as fulfilling commitments from afar, giving support to projects involving Port Talbot in particular. He appears unequivocal about his loyalties and to have both roots and wings.

In 2010 in *Coming Home*, the television series that explores the Welsh origins of famous people, he made it clear that:

> My Welsh roots are everything. It's where I come from, the people I come from, the land I come from. In my own lifetime it's made me who I am.[308]

A sense of identity tends to be sharpened when experienced in relation to other identities and cultures and Sheen has acknowledged that it was only when he left Wales to live in London aged eighteen that he became fully aware of himself as Welsh and what that might signify.

After leaving RADA, Sheen and fellow ex-students Simon

Harris and Natasha Betteridge (who had both also been at WGYTC) set up Thin Language Theatre Company to create more work for Welsh actors and to familiarise London audiences with their work. In 1997 Sheen directed Simon Harris' *Badfinger* (set in a Swansea junk shop) at London's Donmar Warehouse. The cast included Rhys Ifans, Jason Hughes and Port Talbot's Robert Blythe.

Port Talbot's actors appreciate how Sheen has continued to engage with drama locally. Rhys Matthews recalls him coming along to the *Toad of Toad Hall* he directed for WGYTC in Pontardawe in 2011. Sheen was happy to join students in an improvisation session and to be given just one line to speak.

In recent years Sheen has also committed himself to community enterprises that have little or nothing to do with acting. In 2013 he became involved in the furore that resulted from the demolition of the Chartist mural in the centre of Newport, his birthplace. Chartism had been the first nationwide organised movement for democracy in Britain, and Newport was the site of a famous Chartist Rising in 1839. Sheen wrote an open letter to the city's inhabitants condemning the way that the mural had been destroyed without any consultation with them.

He spoke at the annual convention that now takes place on the anniversary of the Rising. Addressing a large audience, his rousing words drew upon actual Chartist phrases such as it being 'a knife and fork question, a bread and cheese question' and sounded like a speech from a latter-day Chartist leader. He not only asked people to remember and celebrate the Chartists and what they stood for but also effectively linked past and present: 'Let us live as though they are all living again, through us.' He appealed to his audience to 'listen to the voices of those on the very edges of our community'.

And like a good Chartist, he had facts to back up his 'hunger politics' argument, pointing out that in 2011 one in six children in Neath Port Talbot County Borough were suffering from severe

poverty: 'If 4,000 children in that one area alone are going to sleep at night hungry and cold, something is terribly wrong'.[309]

He called for a new symbol that would enable the Chartists who had died in the Rising to be remembered. A commission was established to create an appropriate replacement.[310] Sheen also made a television programme marking the 175[th] anniversary of the Newport Rising by following in the footsteps of the marchers, talking to people in valley communities about contemporary issues.[311]

On St David's Day 2015 Sheen addressed a rally in defence of the NHS in Tredegar. Here he invoked the town's most famous son, Nye Bevan. In a rousing speech that reverberated internationally he damned modern politicians for their timidity, calling upon them to: 'By God, believe in something.' Michael Sheen demonstrated what the late Tony Benn and numerous Welsh miners' leaders used to deploy: the power of oratory. Yet in seeking to put the passion back into politics he is also well aware of the dangers of rhetoric, arguing that it needs to be the basis for dialogue that can then lead to change.[312]

He highlights humanitarian projects internationally and in the UK. For example, as a UNICEF Ambassador he has visited Syrian refugees in the Beqaa region on Lebanon's border with Syria and been to Guatemala as part of a campaign to combat violence against children. He works for the Prince's Trust. He is also the Welsh Ambassador for Film Club, a charity founded by the film director Beeban Kidron and has visited schools to talk with young people about the importance and excitement of films, demystifying them and explaining how they changed his life. And he is a Patron of the Drama Association of Wales and holds the RWCMD's International Chair of Drama.

But it is Port Talbot, where his family still lives, that is at the centre of his continued involvement with Wales and Welshness. On 15 July 2008, he was made one of its youngest Freemen of the Borough. The theme of his speech was the importance of a

sense of community. He declared that 'although I no longer live in the community, the community lives in my heart and I've taken Port Talbot with me wherever I've gone. It's been the greatest influence on my life.'

Of course, the cynic might add that such sentiments would be expected in the circumstances and would sound suitably impassioned when delivered by a consummate actor. Yet, if the proof is in the pudding – or, it might be said, the Welsh cakes – there is plenty of evidence to show that Michael Sheen means what he says. In appearance and approachability he remains refreshingly unspoiled by Hollywood even though his every move these days tends to be tracked by the press and social media. And in January 2014 he could be found at the Fostering Network Wales stall at the Aberafan shopping centre, handing out Welsh cakes to passers by.[313] It is where he spent part of his youth. It was also one of the sites for what has been his most significant contribution to the town: *The Passion*, performed over the Easter weekend in 2011.

The initial stimulus for this came from the newly established NTW. Founded in 2009 (six years after its Welsh language equivalent Theatr Genedlaethol Cymru) this English language, pan-Wales, company has no theatre building of its own. Such a situation faced Port Talbot actors for much of the twentieth century although, whereas the lack of a theatre has not been ideal for amateur actors, for NTW it has been liberating, providing the opportunity to situate productions within communities across the country. This has meant taking theatre out to the people rather than vice versa, prompting an organic, engaged response. NTW was given £3 million over three years and a brief to establish the highest quality theatre for the widest possible audience. Thirteen new productions would take place across Wales in its first season. The ambitious programme was announced in 2009.

Sheen was invited to discuss plans with NTW. Apprehensive

that he might be asked to perform *Hamlet*[314] and would have to decline, he was relieved to learn that this was not the case and intrigued by the idea of a theatre map of Wales with plays being performed in different places. He responded by suggesting *The Passion* for a production set in Port Talbot to form the grand finale to the first season. It became the biggest project that NTW had undertaken, with the town becoming the set.

Its focus was no coincidence. Port Talbot already had a tradition of producing a Passion Play and Sheen was inspired by his childhood memory of this. It had originated with Father Sean M. Kearney, Canon of St Theresa's, a modern Catholic church on the Sandfields Estate. Kearney had been a bus driver in Dublin and had entered the priesthood late. Concerned about poverty and social problems in the town, he set up a credit union. He also wanted to get the community involved collectively in a project.[315] What developed became an immensely popular piece of theatre, a passion play called *Behold The Man*. It was performed in Margam for the first time in 1977. Sheen remembered seeing the outdoor event in his childhood and his father's involvement in it.

In 1955 Cyril Jenkins had put on *The Easter Story* at the YMCA with, amongst others, Anthony Hopkins. Margam had already witnessed a Pageant in the 1930s and in 1956 Leo Lloyd had produced the medieval *Everyman* at Margam Abbey. Margam Country Park was deemed a fitting backdrop for this ambitious new undertaking involving large numbers of performers and spectators.

Passion Plays have their origin in Easter Plays performed in medieval Europe but it is the performances at Oberammergau in Bavaria that are best known. The first of these took place in 1634 in the wake of bubonic plague and the midst of the Thirty Years' War. It inaugurated what became a tradition and, stimulated by a revival in the late nineteenth century, this huge undertaking with local amateurs telling the story of the life and

death of Christ in sixteen acts has become an internationally renowned event, taking place once a decade. The last production was in 2010, involved more than 2,000 people and was enacted between May and October on 102 days with one performance daily lasting for five hours.

The Port Talbot Passion Play was also a community event. The scriptwriter of *Behold The Man* was Leo Arthurs, a local actor and playwright who had already written plays for the radio, including one about the local Morfa colliery disaster of 1890 in which eighty-seven men had lost their lives. A Port Talbot Passion Play Association was created and the original committee underwrote the first production. The inspiring Ina D. Jones was the producer and director for the first ten years and then became its Life President.[316] She had long been active in local drama. *Behold The Man* was repeated two years running. It was very successful but expensive to mount (Glamorgan County Council owned Margam Park) so the decision was taken to stage it biennially after that. Anthony Hopkins was made an honorary vice-president.

The actors rehearsed from Easter to June, then the play ran for eleven nights. There were up to 200 crowd actors, in costumes made by women chapelgoers. Audiences of about 850 attended nightly – it needed to be dark for the crucifixion scene – and although the crowd was under cover, the performers were in the open air. Remarkably, only once, when defeated by lightning, was a performance cancelled. Carol Scott (one of the production team) summed up the performers' spirit when describing Griff John's commitment: 'It could be bucketing down but Griff would walk on as though the sun was shining.'

Back in 1890 the actor and writer Elizabeth Robins (who popularised Ibsen's plays on the London stage and played the first Hedda Gabler in English) had travelled to Oberammergau to report on its Passion Play for the newspaper editor W. T. Stead. She discovered that, although for the world at large the

cast appeared as amateurs drilled to deliver their speeches, they were actually highly experienced. She lodged with the man who played Herod and he told her how he had started with a small part in 1840 and gradually assumed bigger roles over the decades. In the years between each production of the Passion Play they would act in religious plays, modern comedies and classics by Shakespeare, Goethe and Schiller.[317]

Many of the *Behold The Man* performers were also well versed in drama. Narrators like Vida Nelson and John Adams were steeped in amateur dramatics. The poet, publisher and former Borough Reference Librarian Sally Roberts Jones, who had met her husband through the Taibach People's Theatre, participated with him and their three sons between 1977 and 1986.[318] There were a number of performers whose names have already featured in this book. The sister of the actor John Paul Macleod was carried on stage when she was a baby. An angelic-looking Jae Alexander was the first to play the young disciple John. In 1997 Michael Sheen's father was narrating in the second set – by this time there were two casts – Ken Tucker was Judas and Betty Brooks Richards the programme steward. She remembers what a 'wonderful community time it was.'

From 1988 scenes from *Behold The Man* would be performed in town on Good Friday though several events there had unexpected effects. At the Arts Centre David S. Davies who played Jesus (and was known as Dai Jesus) first tried out his final scene when a double-decker bus was passing. To their amazement, passengers glimpsed a man on a cross. On another occasion the police received a phone call about possible National Front marchers drilling in the yard at Central School. They were Roman soldiers from the play, practising their marching.

More than 30,000 attended in the first ten years. Nearly £10,000 was put back into the community every two years and distributed to local causes and charities. The decision was taken

to end the production with the close of the twentieth century. Productions were demanding in terms of time and exertion. Lying in wet grass was beginning to lose its appeal. Playing the thirty-three-year old Jesus at the age of fifty-three suggested that change would soon be needed. The final production took place in 1999, some years after the death of Leo Arthurs and twenty-two years after it had begun.

The Passion was very different. It was part of a production by a national theatre company and the Cornish-based WildWorks, and despite having a vast community cast of about 1,000 with up to another 1,000 involved in some aspect of staging the entire event, there was a small professional core at its heart. It was a one-off enacted across the town over the Easter weekend. It could not really have been repeated. It was free for the thousands who came along, although those eager to be as close as possible could book ahead and for a small fee ensure proximity to the heart of the action.

Sheen is not religiously inclined but does admit that he has long been 'obsessed by the story of Jesus'[319] and the way that it has been hardwired into the educational and wider experiences of people growing up in Britain. *Behold The Man* had been rooted in the Christian tradition and in the process succeeded in bringing Catholics, the Church in Wales and various denominations of Chapel members together in one communal undertaking. As Ina Jones put it, this event was essentially about 'The story of the carpenter of Nazareth',[320] *The Passion* was not a recreation of *Behold The Man*. It was a modern secular tale, albeit one that could satisfy those who chose to interpret it in religious terms.

Sheen's plan was to turn the spotlight on his town and its people, to put at the heart of the story a place that had not had much to celebrate in recent years and to demonstrate, through a narrative that took its cue from the Passion story, that there remained in Port Talbot a vibrant, albeit often conflicted, society

with its own tales to tell. In the way that he involved the local community he was drawing upon and inspired by the tradition of performance that had been so important in twentieth-century Port Talbot. Here there *was* a direct link between *The Passion* with its vast community cast and concept of bringing together somewhat different sections of the community *and* the remarkable community event that had energised so many in Margam Park for so long.

Nine months after *The Passion* Sheen even claimed that he had wanted to see whether it was possible to achieve something akin to Greek theatre:

> a communal thing where people come together to share what's important to them, but at the same time to take part in something slightly mysterious and ritualistic, where you acknowledge and experience something bigger than you, something you can't quite put into words.[321]

Perhaps the fact that the event had been judged a resounding success emboldened him to admit this somewhat ambitious aim.

Sheen was the creative director of the 2011 project and a co-director with Bill Mitchell, the founder of WildWorks. This landscape theatre company was used to immersing itself in local community settings from Cornwall to Cyprus, London and Palestine. *The Passion* had a core of fifteen professional actors including Sheen. They came from the locality – a brave move that could not have worked everywhere – and eleven of them were from Port Talbot itself, actors already encountered in this book.[322] There was no problem casting. As Di Botcher who played the Teacher's mother put it: 'How many towns do you know where you have so many professional actors kicking around?'

But production was also predicated upon a massive input from the local community, involving an army of volunteers. The

story unfolded across the town over seventy-two hours, providing an intense, holistic experience of immersive theatre.

So Sheen, used from WGYTC to working in non-traditional theatre that could also draw upon youth dancers and musicians, and fresh from the final two films in *The Twilight Saga,* was working with two companies deeply committed to site-specific theatre. The majority of the actors had themselves been students at WGYTC and those who hadn't had been there were still exposed to its ethos through ex-WGYTC teachers and lecturers. And to this came the imaginative Welsh poet and writer Owen Sheers whose task was to mould a script for the actors and also produce a book which he would call *The Gospel of Us.* He, like Sheen, immersed himself in the town for months beforehand. What eventually emerged was, as Sheers put it, 'a piece of theatre grown from a conversation with the town and its people'.[323]

Researchers from NTW gathered material and a stall in Aberafan shopping centre encouraged people to jot down memories of what had been lost in the town. Sheen sought out stories from local people and groups and Ken Tucker reckons that he unearthed community groups that many people didn't even know existed. By talking to organisations like Dewis (the Welsh word for choice), a housing project for people coming out of foster care, WGCADA (West Glamorgan Council on Alcohol and Drug Abuse) and Organised Kaos, a circus school working with vulnerable children, Sheen not only found what existed beneath the town's surface that could be incorporated into the project but also shifted his own views and the language he used to describe what he witnessed. An eight-year-old boy from an abusive home articulated his anger by punching people. Seeing how he had changed after a year's help from BRAVE (part of Welsh Women's Aid) was, Sheen told *The Big Issue,* nothing less than a miracle.[324]

What eventually unfolded over the three April days in 2011

retold the familiar and dramatic story of Easter. A sinister and corrupt corporation called, fittingly, ICU wants to dig up a town that has already been decimated by roads and create a second bypass (its Passover Project – there are plenty of puns here). A Resistance group is orchestrating opposition. Against an atmosphere of mounting tension with a female suicide bomber at the beach (the Port Talbot actor Francine Morgan), a local teacher who has been missing for forty days and nights returns, shorn of his memory.

What he does therefore – and the Teacher is played by Sheen – is to ask people to help him by telling their stories. Here is a saviour who listens rather than preaches. God is a roofer who looks down on his kingdom and son from above, a part played by David Davies who had been Jesus in *Behold The Man*. Sheen thought him a very good actor and liked the symbolism. Ken Tucker, Sheen's former teacher, was the Mayor (he had alternated between Judas and Jesus in the old Passion Play).

Through the Teacher the town's story emerges and he gathers his disciples round him. But the power of the Company Man (Sheen's old flatmate Hywel Simons) and ICU (Meyrick Sheen played a dignitary supporting the organisation) ensure that he will be put on trial. He is finally put to death not by some clever, modern invention but as in the gospels, by crucifixion. There is the spectacle of a bleeding, broken man on the cross, complete with a crown of thorns.

All this was interwoven with a showcasing of the local community, using a range of artistic groups and enabling those usually without a voice also to be heard. Thus the ladies' choir Côr Serenata, male voice choirs and trained dancers had vital roles to play but so too did the elderly resident of a care home who sang a solo in pyjamas and dressing gown at 6am on the first day of the performance. The Tata Steel Brass Band made music and a child with cerebral palsy communicated with rhythmic taps. People involved in a training project in

woodwork made the crucifix. Members of Taibach Rugby Club, used to performing in the annual pantomime, now found themselves part of the sinister security force that patrolled and terrorised on behalf of ICU, a sort of modern-day legacy from the Roman Empire.

Discussing Irish site-specific theatre, Shaun Richards has described it as 'a machine for making place from space'.[325] In such theatre the physical surroundings contribute to how the performance is interpreted by the audience. There were interesting choices made for the locations in *The Passion*. Take Tanygroes Street, for example which marked the start of the procession of the cross. The English translation of this street name – Beneath the Cross – makes it appropriate but so too does the fact that local people would be aware that this was where Anthony Hopkins had once lived.

The real-life destruction of one half of Llewellyn Street for the building of the motorway link had literally torn a community in two and left the remaining houses facing concrete stilts and slabs. This has long touched a raw nerve. This episode was incorporated into part of the narrative with the telling of ghost stories (drawing upon Sally Roberts Jones' poetry) that may have served a cathartic role, giving some of those former residents a sense of reclaiming their past through activating the memory of place.

On the Saturday night the Port Talbot version of the Last Supper was played out in the Seaside Social Club (Sandfields Social and Labour Club). Two hundred people attended this. The entertainment included the Manic Street Preachers, who performed three numbers, and the opera singer, local resident Paul Potts.

In an interview with the *Western Mail* some months later Sheen explained the drama of what followed. In a downbeat version of the Garden of Gethsemane he was arrested and put on the back of a flatbed truck in a car park. The Head of the

Secret Police attempted to wring from him a confession that he was the town's leader so that he might be imprisoned then put to death. Thousands were watching and by this time were so caught up in the idea that this was the Teacher that when the Head of Police asked whether they thought he was their leader, they confirmed it and so unwittingly betrayed and condemned him. 'That was the moment', Sheen admitted, 'when I realised this wasn't a play any more.' Now 'the boundary between fiction and reality was totally blurred, which is what I'd always hoped for. It was a devastating moment.'[326]

The climax came, as Owen Sheers put it, 'on a darkening roundabout beside the sea'.[327] A mundane, much used road that runs the length of the seafront was the setting for the crucifixion scene rather than a green hill in the distance. Sheen had already explored the possibility of other, more conventional sites including Aberavon Rugby Club. Although he could have no idea of the numbers involved, a large space was needed. But keeping an audience in the rugby stands would have been akin to conventional theatre in its separation of performers and audience. Part of the power of this event was its interaction with the public, the way that the crowd could shift how scenes unfolded. Their collusion was vital and some proximity essential. In a town that had been cruelly dissected by roads it seemed apposite that the people should re-appropriate space normally used by cars.

In advance of the event Michael Sheen, the other actors and all involved had understandably been apprehensive. Part of the challenge and excitement of this type of theatre is the element of the unknown. It was, as NTW's Lucy Davies put it, 'so seat of the pants'.[328] Sheen produced an initial synopsis and there was a lot of improvisational work. Owen Sheers had to produce speeches at speed. Only when it happened and all, audience included, lived it together could it really be tested and said to work.

During rehearsals in pouring rain Sheen warned that although

there might be thousands, they should be prepared for it to be very different: 'There may be Mum and Dad and a dog'.[329] But, when the time came, fears gave way to the realisation that this was becoming a major event. People came from near and far. Dylan Moore wrote in *Planet*: 'This wasn't Wales on the world stage. This was the world on Wales' stage.'[330] Numbers built from a few hundred at dawn on Good Friday to many thousands. Sheen, no stranger to football crowds, said afterwards that he would always remember walking along the beach later that morning (in character) and 'seeing more people than I've ever seen in my life'.[331] An estimated 15–20,000[332] attended the final scene on Sunday night. For those who believed in miracles, in place of rain was glorious sunshine all weekend. So hot was it that it seemed more like the Middle East than south Wales.

It was both exhilarating and tough being part of the audience. At times it felt like being on a gigantic film set. Walking down Station Road in the centre of town you might spy a 'Missing' poster advertising the fact that a local teacher had been missing for a month. Despite the vast crowds there was no actual police presence. However, because fiction and reality were so blurred, there was no need given the sinister omniscient presence of ICU's thuggish security forces.

Since the fundamental story is such a familiar one, even picking it up part way through was less problematic than it would have been in many shows, despite the fact that there were unexpected elements that gave it a modern twist. Comprehension was aided by Sheers producing daily limited edition booklets that outlined the narrative to date.

The mounting tension of the story and the involvement of all made it unlike any other event. Matthew Aubrey, who was one of the core cast, says he has never seen so many grown men cry. Bloodied and battered after being incarcerated and beaten up, the Teacher dragged the cross for miles in searing heat

accompanied by crowds and crowds of people chanting 'Come on, Michael'. The final scene was due to start at 10pm on Aberafan Seafront. Many thousands had gathered. It was another hour before the exhausted Teacher reached the spot. The pubs had been open all day and it was a time of heightened tension. We were packed in tightly. It could have turned very nasty. And much could have gone wrong with getting Sheen high on the cross and feigning his death (though he had been to Oberammergau and discussed the crucifixion scene with their Jesus).

Instead there was a rapt audience. As darkness fell, the pinpricks of light from a myriad of mobile phone cameras reminded me of the candles held aloft by the thousands of operagoers who perch on the steps of the amphitheatre in Verona to watch night-time performances. At Aberafan popular memory came into play in a remarkable scene that must have been bizarre for the many visitors. The dying Teacher whose past had been erased cried out 'I remember' and there followed an incantation of past people and places that had an electrifying impact. As each word was uttered so cheers resounded from those for whom it was significant. From Beach Hill and The Regent to Selwyn Jenkins and the Forge Road Baths, each stirred a glorious 'collective alchemy'.[333]

A haunting lament that had been sung earlier when the Teacher's wounds had been treated by his mother and other women (including Sheen's own mother) was heard once more. Then, in a final transcendent act after he had been crucified and all had been declared finished, the Teacher appeared again momentarily in a new guise, uttering the words 'It has Begun'.

One reviewer commented that 'After this breathtaking act of theatrical magic, Michael Sheen can book himself in for local sanctification'.[334] One reason why he has earned so much respect is that he never took short cuts. In the role of the Teacher he really did spend a night in a cell and slept the

previous night on the mountainside.

Although Michael Sheen, local lad, had made his personal journey and gone far away to a much more glamorous world, he had returned home too many times in recent years to justify the biblical label of the Prodigal Son. This was not somebody who whizzed in and out and delegated to others but who visited people personally. Sheen's approach as they prepped the performance was one of mucking in like anybody else. The actors also appreciated his adoption of a round table rather than head of table approach in rehearsals. Rhys Matthews (who played one of the Teacher's sons) echoed others when he described this experience as 'the best job I've ever done'.

Owen Sheers admitted in 2012 that he found it 'one of the most incredible experiences of my life so far' and that it had helped him to develop more 'socially involved writing'.[335] His powerful verse-drama *Pink Mist* about three young soldiers who experienced war in Afghanistan followed. It was performed and recorded for BBC Radio 4 (which had commissioned it) that year in Bristol. Port Talbot's Jordan Bernarde played Taff, one of the three soldiers. *Pink Mist* won the 2014 Wales Book of the Year.[336]

Sheen's verdict on *The Passion* sounded as though he possessed a crystal ball: 'It will undoubtedly be the most significant thing in my career, I know that, but also, the most significant thing in my life'.[337] He did, though, qualify that second claim with 'probably', and he explained that it taught him about what was possible both in terms of theatre and in empowering a community. For NTW producer Lucy Davies who had met Michael Sheen and Owen Sheers at the outset to discuss possibilities, the result was 'an alchemical weekend' when 'you know that you were part of something historic.'[338]

The reviews in the national and international press were overwhelmingly positive. Lyn Gardner in the *Guardian* (the London-based paper, not the local one, which had ceased to

exist) awarded the event five stars and commented that although Oberammergau was the world's most famed Passion Play, 'it's hard to believe any version can have the heart and soul of Port Talbot's one-off, multi-platform production'.[339] Her account of the 'spectacle of angels on fiery bicycles, ghosts, snipers perched on the shopping centre, and shrines to lost futures' argues that here was 'so much more than an epic piece of street theatre' and that being there was 'like watching a town discovering itself through a shared act of creation'. For the *Independent* reviewer the three days amounted to 'the most extraordinary piece of community-specific theatre' she had ever seen.[340]

Inevitably there was the occasional dissenting voice. Wary of what he saw as an example of a demotic populist reading of the Bible, the critic Philip French felt it patronising.[341] However, his assessment was based on the film version of the event entitled *The Gospel Of Us*, and he left the cinema before the final crucifixion scene. Moreover, his paper the *Observer* had earlier been responsible for describing what went on in Port Talbot as one of the outstanding events of the decade.[342] Perhaps most importantly, as Dave McKean [343] (multi-talented director of the film) admitted, for local people '*The Passion* was all about being there, live, and a film can never touch that.'[344] McKean admits too that the film would be not be easy and was 'for people who enjoy a puzzle'. It could be argued that for anybody, not just local people, the film is best appreciated as a supplement to rather than a substitution for the original event.

The feature film *The Gospel Of Us* was made by Film Agency Wales and NTW.[345] During the weekend of *The Passion* there had been ten cameras recording the event as discreetly as possible. Making a two-hour film out of many hours of drama with a vast, live audience was a huge challenge though it also provided an opportunity for some extra scenes (especially before the final drama of the crucifixion) and special effects. Although

at the time the press cameras and sea of mobile phones had threatened to get in the way of the filming and even the performance itself, this proved useful in that some of the clips on YouTube were incorporated into the film.

Sheen has commented how the gospels told the Easter story in different ways and so too was that Easter weekend in 2011 experienced in various forms and formats. The BBC made two documentaries.[346] Social media ensured that the stories and pictures were whisked round the world and a website framed as a local blog included an alternative reality game.[347] Owen Sheers' three booklets were reissued as a book. One year on at Easter 2012, to coincide with the world premiere of *The Gospel Of Us* introduced by Sheen at the Apollo Cinema on the seafront, a three-day multimedia Memory Exhibition was held at the Aberafan shopping centre. The pubic was invited to scan photographs and film their favourite memories and swap stories.

Reviews of *The Passion* had lauded the transformative nature of the event. Lyn Gardner's ended with the comment that 'Port Talbot's future starts the very second *The Passion* ends'.[348] Whether the town's fortunes have been turned around since then is debatable but what can't be denied is the radical intervention and commitment by the actor Michael Sheen to an uplifting experience. It prompted Gardner to describe Port Talbot for those three days at Easter 2011 as one of the happiest places on Earth.

So is there something in the water?

Although experimental and in many ways unique, *The Passion* can also be seen as encapsulating the creative tradition built up over the years in Port Talbot, fusing the amateur and the professional. Orchestrated by NTW and WildWorks, it brought together the town's most recent international film star and a selection of other indigenous actors alongside amateur performers and community groups in what Owen Sheers has called 'A maelstrom of an experience in which the audience would be both witness and participant'.[349] It took place in a venue that might not seem to outsiders the obvious home for the acting profession. Yet Port Talbot has produced a disproportionate number of actors since the 1930s. Why is this so, and what does the future look like for its actors?

There is no simple answer. A few of the actors considered here, for example Peg Entwistle and Ronald Lewis, were born in the town but not essentially shaped by it. Nevertheless, an important factor for the majority of Port Talbot's professional actors is one much cited in Welsh history generally: an appreciation of education. In the depressed inter-war years in particular there was a stress on the importance of widening horizons and developing opportunities through study, whether at school, in Eisteddfodau or in adult learning. The work of the Glamorgan Education Committee and a belief in what might be called *The Corn is Green* effect – Emlyn Williams' play of 1938 in which a teacher recognises and develops latent Oxford material in a young Welsh collier – did make a difference.

In Port Talbot this coalesced in the form of Philip Burton.

Here was a gifted man, from a mining background, who possessed great skills as a teacher. He imparted his enthusiasm for the stage to others. Burton's nurturing of raw talent and the vital contacts he developed and continued to cultivate within the BBC, made the world of difference. The promising young people he taught at the Sec in the 1930s and early 1940s were testimony to this. Richard Burton became his best-known success. But, as we have seen, there were others too, encouraged to explore literature, language and drama in particular, who took up professional or semi-professional careers as actors or became immersed in amateur theatre. The Appendix reveals a significant cluster of actors born in the 1920s.

The town's early stars are beginning to receive attention. In March 2014 Bryn Residents Action Group persuaded the council to name a street after their local actor. Owen Jones Way/Ffordd Owen Jones helps to recognise the gifted Shakespearean actor who died during the Second World War.[350]

After Richard Burton died in 1984 a memorial service was held in Bethel Chapel, Pontrhydyfen. But despite biographies by two of his brothers, and a tribute function at the Afan Lido in 1985 orchestrated by Bryn Thomas, the town did not mark publicly anniversaries of his birth or death. In 1998, however, on what would have been his seventy-third birthday, a new plaque was unveiled outside 2, Dan-y-Bont, the house where he had been born in Pontrhydyfen. His widow Sally Burton attended, as did Graham Jenkins, sole survivor of the siblings, and there was media speculation about his wish for his brother's remains to be brought home to Wales.[351] In 2006 a black marble memorial in Welsh was unveiled close to Burton's parents' grave declaring that he was a 'Seren Cymru a'r Byd' (Star of Wales and the World).

The gift of Burton's diaries and papers by his widow to Swansea University resulted in the university's archives being

named in his memory (in 2010) and the establishment of a Richard Burton Centre for the Study of Wales with an annual lecture. In 2012 came the publication of his surviving diaries by Professor Chris Williams. Further projects are underway.

Chairing the university's Richard Burton Advisory Board, Professor Hywel Francis, MP for Aberafan between 2001 and 2015, has played a key role in promoting the memory of Burton in his constituency. Neath Port Talbot Council has developed two Richard Burton walking trails. On the Birthplace Trail in Pontrhydyfen you can listen to him reading a Dylan Thomas poem and hear a passage from his recording of *Under Milk Wood*. The Childhood Trail in Taibach features a flowerbed (called 'lights, camera, action') in the Memorial Park. Here are displayed the last lines of one of Burton's own unpublished poems.[352] In 2013, when the *Western Mail's* campaign to see the actor represented in the Hollywood Walk of Fame was realised (his star was unveiled by Michael Sheen), Neath Port Talbot held a Richard Burton month in November. Events included the annual 10-kilometre Richard Burton fun run from Cwmafan Community Centre, sponsored by Tata Steel.[353]

So the town's acting heritage is being writ large in its achievements. Guests at the Afan Lodge Hotel in Duffryn Rhondda, formerly the Miners' Institute where Richard Jenkins performed, can stay in the Richard Burton room complete with pictures and a scrapbook detailing the actor's local connections. Blanco's Hotel and Restaurant in Aberafan has a large Michael Sheen Suite for private functions. Burton, Hopkins, Sheen, Brydon and Di Botcher feature in a mural of the town's famous figures that includes sporting heroes such as the international rugby player James Hook.

And might there also be something in the voice of those Port Talbot actors? Is there a clue to the town's success in the plangent tones that emerge from the fusion of that local accent with training for the stage? And it has been a training that has

not only come from drama school. The young Burton who, thanks to Philip Burton, set the Gold Standard, had also been encouraged and aided by other dedicated figures in the town, most notably Meredith Jones and Leo Lloyd. The promotion of an experimental youth centre with a drama section was a big asset. This, allied to talent in music and performance fostered by the chapels and expressed in amateur choirs and drama groups, as well as the development of a YMCA, created an atmosphere in which a taste for the stage could flourish. Of course, Port Talbot was not alone here. Indeed, the existence of a vibrant tradition in which drama groups frequently competed with each other, whether in Eisteddfodau or drama contests across south Wales and beyond, helped to develop this further.

Port Talbot, however, had an advantage. And that was its geography. It is well positioned between two major locations: Swansea and Cardiff. It is and has been easy to get away by train or by car. A comparable industrial town like Llanelli further west lacked such access. Philip Burton could take those boys to the BBC in Cardiff without difficulty. Being on the coastal plain, *Port* Talbot looks outwards. As an employer of miners, workers on the harbour and steel workers the district has long been used to taking in people from further afield. It is not an insular place cut off from the wider world. It has been sizeable enough to make its mark for many decades as a distinct borough, yet small enough to retain a sense of community that is akin to that in a valleys town but with better transport. Doug Rees has noted how it has 'never failed to produce artistry and a deep love of the town' and that 'there is still a village feel to a town atmosphere'. This has served its actors well.

The iconic steelworks make it instantly recognisable. Although only one amongst the UK plants (and now a shadow of its former self though still, vitally, in operation) it lies in a powerful position by the sea. There is also a mountainous

backdrop. As Owen Sheers has remarked, it is 'inherently a dramatic town'.[354]

Its Otherness has been expressed in various ways. When I was a child living more or less opposite one of the entrances to the Works, Port Talbot was very much a Company Town. The continental shift system created continuous shifts with three rush hours in every twenty-four hours, one at 10pm. Traffic queues were exacerbated in those pre-motorway days by the Level Crossing that held up cars and buses right in the middle of town.

For Michael Sheen the fact that Port Talbot never could be mistaken for suburbia adds to its edgy appeal. He likes to point out that the beach gave Terry Gilliam the idea for what became the cult film *Brazil*.[355] Add to this what he calls the 'dark energy' of the landscape, an indigenous repartee and the influence of Burton and Hopkins – never safe, cosy figures – and there is a potent mix that, for Sheen and others, helps to stimulate ideas for interpreting and playing parts on stage and screen. As we have seen, emulation is also an important ingredient in understanding how and why the town has developed such a proud tradition of acting.

The fact that Port Talbot has been much derided by others as an eyesore seems also to have engendered a sense of loyalty and defensiveness that accentuates a pride in place. In the 1960s the writer Gwyn Thomas described it as 'a stretch of incomparable industrial foulness'.[356] Labelling it as 'Giro City' can have its uses but it also runs the risk of simplifying and generalising. It is akin to George Orwell's portrayal of Wigan in the 1930s, predicated upon highlighting the Lancashire town's worst lodging house and slums.[357] Port Talbot may be an industrial town in decline with inevitable attendant problems but that is not the whole story.

One Chance, the 2013 film of the story of Paul Potts, shows how it can be represented as a dead-end place. The rags to riches story tells how the gifted singer battled with low self-

esteem, bullying and limited horizons to win *Britain's Got Talent* and so get propelled into the limelight. It uses the town to show his 'humble' background and conveniently ignores the fact that Potts was from the Bristol area, went to school there, gained a B.A. degree in Humanities from University College Plymouth and was a Liberal Democrat City Councillor in Bristol. He became the manager of a Carphone Warehouse store in Bridgend, not an assistant in Port Talbot. But perhaps the most interesting aspect of his real-life story is that the immensely successful international star and his wife still live in Port Talbot.

There are manifold explanations as to why individuals might decide to become actors. Many, across time and place, have stressed the sense of belonging that engaging in drama has engendered for them, providing a vital sense of community. One young Port Talbot actor told me that he would probably be in prison if it weren't for acting. It provided a vital outlet and focus for him. Simply getting away from a life in the Works or out of work has to be a possible explanation for some. Another actor, Kyle Rees, explained that he was seeking something that saved him from a life labouring on building sites. Inspiring teachers at Sandfields and Gorseinon College channelled his interests in the direction of drama (though much of his passion when young was for rugby). An acting career might not provide the security of a permanent job but it suggested opportunities. What is striking, though, is that he and other actors nevertheless retain a fervent attachment to Port Talbot even whilst being based in London or elsewhere, and some have returned to live there.

The amateur tradition continues but is diminished and challenged by rising costs[358] and dwindling audiences. During the years immediately following the Second World War it was possible to attend productions by at least a dozen amateur groups in the town. But that was before television secured its ineluctable grip. Yet television, as we have seen, has also been beneficial, since it has provided real and expanded

opportunities for Port Talbot's actors. Radio drama offered openings for some of the town's early performers and it too gives work to today's professional actors. However, as Dame Judi Dench and Timothy West have recently observed, the demise of a repertory system where many stage actors learned their trade, is to be regretted, especially at a time when funding training is problematic.[359]

In the past those wanting to make their mark needed to leave Wales. Now NTW beckons, along with television companies and film and video developments such as Pinewood in Cardiff and the Bay Studios on the Port Talbot side of Swansea. It was here that the global television series *Da Vinci's Demons* originated, a reimagining of the life of Leonardo, partly filmed at Margam Castle but also engaging some of the Port Talbot actors, for example Kyle Rees and Jordan Bernarde. Attached to the studios is Europe's largest individual film stage.[360] Sustained employment in the profession is always difficult to achieve but at least openings within Wales have improved for actors in recent years, and Cardiff's RWCMD is flourishing. The *Observer* on St David's Day 2015 declared that it was a heyday for Welsh actors.[361]

It would nevertheless be foolish to ignore or even minimise some very real problems. The corrosive effects of long-term unemployment and related issues such as drug dependency continue to dog the town. The 2005 Welsh Index of Multiple Deprivation identified Sandfields West as one of the most disadvantaged electoral wards in the country.[362] *The Passion* revealed something of the town's underbelly, though it also suggested that efforts were being made from within the community to mitigate the worst effects of deprivation.

The recession has clearly taken its toll. Di Botcher recently played a role she would rather not have had to undertake: she opened a Food Bank in the town. Although the steel industry in Port Talbot had weathered the recession of 1990–1, the economic downturn from 2008 saw its owners, the Indian

multinational company Tata, drastically reduce its European production. A new blast furnace remained mothballed. There are fears that pollution is getting worse, not better. Natural Resources Wales and the Health and Safety Executive have a busy time dealing with reports of black dust emissions and orange dust clouds.[363] The town has long had alarmingly high cancer rates. There is some local concern too that planning permission has been given to a fracking company for a well to target coal *and* shale deposits close to Pontrhydyfen.

In 2009 the town's sports and entertainments complex the Afan Lido was destroyed by fire. Taibach Library no longer has paid employees; it is kept going by volunteers. Local authority cuts are affecting teaching provision at Gower College and other crucial providers of further education that have been so vital for developing drama. The proposed reorganisation of local authorities in Wales adds to uncertainty about the future.

Glan Afan School has lost its drama department – something Michael Sheen has condemned publicly – though at least its annual show has been revived. WGYTC had its funding cut in 2012. More recently it was in danger of losing its entire grant from Swansea Council. This has not happened to date but funding for 2015–16 has been cut by 20 per cent and it will need to apply competitively for grant funding in future. The threat of cuts undermines the decades of commitment to arts education that created vital opportunities for the individuals featured in this book and challenges the important role that drama plays in the wellbeing of communities.

The Plaza Cinema, cherished by the town for many decades, has remained boarded up with a sign proclaiming 'Coming Soon'. How soon, people ask, *is* soon? Was Port Talbot's happiness just for three sunny Easter days in 2011?

Yet all is not gloom and doom. Baglan Energy Park and the opening of Swansea University's new Bay Campus at Crymlyn Burrows are positive developments to the west. The latter will

include a Great Hall where a mosaic portrait of Richard Burton, commissioned by Sally Burton, will face in the direction of Port Talbot. Work has finally begun on a new Afan Lido on the site of the derelict bowling alley at Hollywood Park (another of those erstwhile genuflections to American society). And at the time of writing (April 2015) ambitious regeneration plans for the area around the railway station, partially funded by the Welsh Government, include the seventy-five-year-old Plaza being turned into 'An Arts Centre of Excellence' encompassing a theatre suitable for professional and amateur productions and a digital film studio.[364] This had been a wish expressed at the time of *The Passion*.

Despite the ominous shadow of continuing concern over funding, WGYTC, now in its fortieth year is – at present at least – still going strong. Godfrey Evans believes that student ambition, appetite and discipline are as impressive as ever and that standards are, if anything, higher. Vivienne Buckley is its artistic director. She has also established with Rhys Matthews (Matthew Rees of Gower College) a self-funded Graduate Theatre Company.[365]

Just eight out of the fifty Port Talbot actors listed in the Appendix are female. The majority of the mentors and role models in the past were male. In recent years, however, there have been more female drama teachers locally and a feminisation of the drama student population generally. Until 1993 just one third of RADA students in a year group were female. One of their students graduating in 2015 is Rosie Sheehy, ex-Glan Afan and WGYTC. She will appear in Eugene O'Neill's *The Hairy Ape* at the Old Vic where Port Talbot's Owen Jones had performed in the 1930s.

At Dyffryn, where Philip Burton and later Selwyn Davies were so revered, the subject leader for drama is the popular Caroline Michael, another product of WGYTC. At Sandfields Helen John radiates enthusiasm and energy. She has taught there for

seventeen years and is currently developing (with a former colleague in music) a small stage school. She is in the honourable tradition of Port Talbot teachers who have also remained active within the wider amateur dramatics community.

There are, however, enormous changes on the horizon. In the summer of 2016, Sandfields, Glan Afan and Briton Ferry's Cwrt Sart comprehensives will close and be replaced by Bae Baglan (Baglan Bay) a 'super school' with 1,000 pupils. First class facilities are promised including a purpose-built drama studio and two large fully equipped performance spaces.

It is only right that this book should end with teachers of drama and educational plans. They and amateurs committed to drama like Cyril Jenkins and Leo Lloyd provide a vital key to why Port Talbot has had such a vibrant tradition. Allied to policies that have fostered opportunities and creativity in the arts for young people in particular they have made the most of their resources and helped to make possible the commitment to drama that has characterised this town since the inter-war years.

Port Talbot has indeed produced world-famous, superlative actors. Each generation has been a vital stimulus to the next but it has not been a case of isolated geniuses keen to turn their backs on a rough town. The 'something in the water' isn't accidental. The town's superstars, like all the others, need to be seen as part of a careful shaping of innate talent by dedicated individuals and institutions, not cut off from local drama but emerging out of this crucible.

The old Sec divided its pupils into four houses named after medieval figures. Its modern version Dyffryn Comprehensive has three houses: Burton, Emmanuel and Hopkins and has long held Eisteddfodau on a house basis. The Lower School Library (in the old Sec Building) is now called the Philip and Richard Burton Library. Hopefully, in time, Port Talbot will recognise more of the heroes behind the scenes who have helped to make it a town of stars as well as steel.

Fifty Port Talbot Actors

(Names, if different from stage names, are in brackets)

MARC ANTOLIN: Sandfields (head boy), Port Talbot Stage School, WGYTC, Arts Ed. Acting credits include the original RSC production of *Matilda* and performances in Chichester Festival Theatre such as *Taken at Midnight* (with transfer to Theatre Royal, Haymarket). Films include *Love Actually* (2003).

PHILLIP ARRAN: Mark Jermin Stage School, Gorseinon College. Musical theatre. West End work includes *Priscilla Queen of the Desert*. In Mal Pope's *Amazing Grace* (2005).

MATTHEW AUBREY: Sandfields, Gorseinon, RWCMD. See Chapter 4.

JORDAN BERNARDE (Piles): Sandfields, Gorseinon, WGYTC, RWCMD. Work includes William M. Hoffmann's *As Is* at the Finborough Theatre, London and TV film *First Light*.

DOUGLAS BLACKWELL 1924–2009: County. Television credits include *The Avengers* and *Dixon of Dock Green* and films spanning 1960s to 1990s including *The Ipcress File* (1965) and *Robin Hood: Prince of Thieves* (1991).

ROBERT BLYTHE: Arts Ed. See Chapter 4.

PHILIP BOND: Born Staffordshire but spent much of childhood in Blaengwynfi and Blaengarw. Central, Oxford University. Returned to Wales 1978. See Chapter 4.

DI BOTCHER: Dyffryn, WGYTC, Warwick University, Douglas Webber. See Chapter 4.

STEPHEN BOTCHER 1956–2000: Dyffryn, RWCMD. In

Absolute Hell and *The Merry Wives of Windsor* at the National 1995–6.

ROB BRYDON (Robert Brydon Jones): RWCMD. See Chapters 4 and 5.

DENNIS BURGESS 1926–80: Sec. See Chapter 5.

RICHARD BURTON CBE (Jenkins): 1925–84. Sec. See Chapters 1, 4 and 5.

MICHELLE BUTT: Sandfields, The Bristol Old Vic Theatre School. Television and film work as well as extensive experience in English theatre including *Cider with Rosie*, Birmingham Rep National Tour; Bristol Old Vic's *Dona Rosita the Spinster*, and *Spring Awakening* at London's Young Vic.

NORMAN COMER: Glan Afan. RADA. See Chapter 4.

MICHAEL CONWAY: Dyffryn/Porthcawl Comprehensive, Gorseinon, Arts Ed. Musical Theatre. First professional show was *Fiddler on the Roof*. See Chapter 3.

JEREMY DAVID (Fussell): Glan Afan, RWCMD after working in a bank. TV includes *Casualty*. Part in the film *The Crumbs of Happiness* (1998).

DAI 'DWSH' DAVIES: 1920s–c. 2000. Eastern School. Amateur Entertainer in local shows and pantomimes. Toured clubs. Specialised in mime. Worked for Taibach Co-operative stores, initially as a milkman. Semi-professional. Extra and walk-on parts in more than 100 feature films/TV including *Grand Slam* (1978).

CATHERINE DOLAN (Phyllis Dolan): 1920s–91. Sec, RADA, Birmingham Rep. Lead in Bernard Shaw's *Mrs Warren's Profession* at Dublin Drama Festival 1961, followed by European tour. Theatre in West End (was Rosie Probert in *Under Milk Wood*). and in United States. Radio plays (BBC Third Programme, also Welsh Home Service) and TV (Armchair Theatre).

IVOR EMMANUEL: 1927–2007: See Chapter 5.

PEG ENTWISTLE (Millicent Lilian): 1908–32: See Chapter 1.

BERNARD M. FOX: Son of English stage actors who moved to Wales just before he was born in 1927. Acting from age of fourteen. Post-war in Rep and Whitehall Farces. By 1960s in Hollywood. Recreated a Victorian musical hall in Santa Monica. TV includes *The Man from U.N.C.L.E.* Thirty film credits 1956–2004 including *Titanic*.

JUSTIN GOLDING: Glan Afan, WGYTC. Member of National Youth Theatre of Great Britain. Springboard Theatre Company. UK TV walk-on parts before moving to US where he has directed plays. Teacher, screenwriter and director of films such as *The Gods of Circumstances* (2009), in which he also has a part.

DANIEL GRAHAM (Williams): Dyffryn, Gorseinon, RWCMD. Actor and singer. In *Sky Hawk* for Clwyd Theatr Cymru, and *Sweeney Todd* at Chichester (West End transfer), *Gulliver's Travels* on Radio 4.

JENNIFER HILL: LAMDA in mid-1950s. In Port Talbot Drama Club before professional theatre. Worked in Rep and for National Theatre, Clwyd Theatr Cymru etc. TV includes three years in *Crossroads* and *Softly Softly*. Films include *Giro City* (1982).

Sir ANTHONY HOPKINS CBE: RWCMD, RADA. See Chapters 2, 4 and 5.

DEREK HUTCHINSON: Sandfields, WGYTC, King's College, London. In *King Lear* (Donmar Warehouse) and Chichester Festival productions, including *Amadeus*. Films include *V for Vendetta* and *Stage Beauty*. Various TV appearances from *Stella* to *The Casual Vacancy* (2015).

BRINLEY JENKINS 1926–2001: Sec, Monmouthshire Training College, Caerleon. Taught for seven years. Amateur theatre acting, writing and producing plays. In 1953 joined

BBC Welsh Repertory Company (£9 weekly salary). Films include *Rebecca's Daughters* (1992). Acting for the BBC in hundreds of English and Welsh dramas up to 1989.

GAZ JENKINS: Gorseinon, Blackpool and Fylde College. Based in Blackpool as singer and actor. Theatre tour with Steel Wasp Theatre Company in *Moll Flanders*. In 2008 founded RED2 Theatre Company.

MARSHALL JONES (Michael): County, RADA (won Forbes Robertson scholarship). Amateur theatre turned professional. TV work included *Crossroads*. In horror films such as *Cry of the Banshee* (1970) and *Scream and Scream Again* (1970).

(Thomas) **OWEN JONES** 1914–42: Sec, RADA. See Chapter 1.

PHILIP JOSEPH: Sandfields, Manchester Polytechnic. Rep. Liverpool Everyman Theatre. TV includes BBC series *To Serve Them All My Days* and part of Joe Gargery in *Great Expectations*. Produces. Guest tutor for National Theatre.

LUKE JOYCE: Sandfields, Gorseinon, Central, Middlesex University. Musical theatre. A co-founder of Thrust Theatre 2007 to showcase work in progress. In *The Unknown Soldier* for TV.

GARY LAGDEN (Williams): Sandfields, WGYTC, New College. See Chapter 4.

DARREN LAWRENCE: Sandfields, WGYTC, Central. Actor and director. Theatre work includes *The Village Social* on tour with NTW. TV work includes *Lipstick on Your Collar* mini-series, *Nuts and Bolts* and *Cucumber* (2015).

RONALD LEWIS 1928–82: RADA. See Chapter 4.

JOHN-PAUL MACLEOD: Sylvia Young Drama School, London, Gorseinon. In 2014 he appeared in an award-winning science fiction film, *The Machine*.

RHYS MATTHEWS (Matthew Rees): Glan Afan, WGYTC,

RADA. Actor/Tutor and runs a bakery. In film *Night of the Living Dead: Resurrection* (2012).

(Leonard) **BRUCE MAYNE** 1926–68: Glan Afan. Taught in Port Talbot Central Junior School. Active in amateur dramatics acting and production (e.g. Port Talbot Drama Club and Little Theatre, also dramas with young people (e.g. Pontrhydyfen County Youth Club). In the 1950s and 1960s acted in dramas for the Welsh Home Service, including several plays by Gwyn Thomas, as well as readings and interviews (e.g. for *Good Morning Wales*). In 1967 he joined the BBC staff as a producer but was killed in a car accident the following year en route to work in Cardiff.

EVAN R. MORGAN 1914-1993: Sec. Teacher/Headmaster. Mountain School/Sandfields Junior. Dramatist and actor in Welsh and English-language plays in Port Talbot and on radio. Semi-professional.

FRANCINE MORGAN: Sandfields, WGYTC, Central. Morgan and Owen Teale acted in the Radio 4 play *Fallen* in 2001 by Philip Palmer, ex-Sandfields pupil. See Chapter 3.

CHRISTINA MODESTOU: Sandfields, Gorseinon, Arts Ed. Musical Theatre includes *We Will Rock You*.

SIÂN OWEN: Glan Afan, RWCMD. See Chapter 4.

KRISTIAN PHILLIPS: Glan Afan, Gorseinon, Bristol Old Vic. In *The Tempest* (Lord Chamberlain's Men). TV includes *Wizards versus Aliens*.

RAYMOND PIKE: Eastern Schools, Taibach Youth Centre in early 1940s. On professional stage by 1950s. Moved to London. Emigrated to Australia.

JOHN (Morgan) **REES** 1927–94: Central. See Chapter 4.

KYLE REES: Sandfields, Gorseinon, Royal Scottish Academy of Music and Drama. See Chapter 4.

DAVID RHYS-MORRIS: Mark Jermin Stage School, Academy of Musical Theatre, Wales. Actor/singer. TV includes *Hope and Glory*. Part in *The Testimony of Taliesin Jones*. Founded Fame Factory Theatre School.

MICHAEL SHEEN OBE: Glan Afan, WGYTC, RADA. See Chapters 3, 4 and 6.

GARETH SNOOK: Sandfields, WGYTC, Central. Specialises in musical theatre. Has worked with Stephen Sondheim, Trevor Nunn and Andrew Lloyd Webber. Reprised his role of André in *Phantom of the Opera* at the Albert Hall for the 25[th] anniversary production filmed by Universal Pictures. Lead in *The Rink* in West End premiere. In *Made in Dagenham*, Adelphi Theatre, London (2015). In film of *Les Misérables* and on stage at London's Palace Theatre.

DAVID REES TALBOT (David Jones): Glan Afan, RWCMD. TV includes *Score*. Radio voice-overs.

This list does not claim to be complete. Information is based on author's interviews and communications as well as *South Wales Evening Post*; *Port Talbot Guardian; Glamorgan Gazette, Western Mail*; Leslie Evans Papers in West Glamorgan Archives; BBC Written Archives Centre, Caversham Park, Reading; the Internet Movie database: www.imdb.com and www.walesonline.co.uk.

NOTES

Unattributed quotes and comments come from my recorded interviews and other communications with the individuals concerned. Abbreviations: GG (*Glamorgan Gazette*); NLW (National Library of Wales, Aberystwyth); PTG (*Port Talbot Guardian*); RBP (Richard Burton Papers, Richard Burton Archives, Swansea University); SWEP (*South Wales Evening Post*), WGA (West Glamorgan Archives, Swansea).

[1] *Guardian* 17 August 2007.

[2] Ibid 18 August 2005. This poll was in association with the wine makers Mouton Cadet. In 2014 Burton and Hopkins featured in the Top 50 Greatest Welsh People in History. Aneurin Bevan topped the list with Hopkins at number 46 and Burton at 29, though it was acknowledged that 'at his peak, he [Burton] would have been the most famous Welshman'.

[3] Figures from Port Talbot include Andrew Vicari, joint-second in the list of the world's wealthiest artists; David Carpanini, whose paintings focus on Tuscany and his native Afan Valley and Lord Howe of Aberavon (Geoffrey Howe), son of a local solicitor. The president of the South Wales Miners' Federation and Rhondda MP William Abraham (Mabon) was born at Cwmafan in 1842 and Dic Penderyn, martyr of the Merthyr Rising, is buried in St Mary's, Aberafan. Professor Chris Evans, biotechnology entrepreneur, is Port Talbot-born. In 1927 Martin Lloyd-Jones, assistant to the king's physician, exchanged his medical career for a decade in the Forward Movement mission at Bethlehem Evangelical Church, Sandfelds.

[4] Lynne Rees, *Real Port Talbot*, Seren, 2013, p. 9: a lively, informative account.

[5] The list contains seven actors, four singers, one actor/singer, one artist, one comedian, a radio presenter and two dance acts. The singer Katherine Jenkins is from Neath. Bonnie Tyler from nearby Skewen and Max Boyce have the Freedom of the County Borough of Neath Port Talbot. The TDM Stage School and Dance Academy is run by the choreographer Terry Michael, who took NU-Skool and Pre-Skool dancers to the finals of TV's *Britain's Got Talent*.

[6] This book concentrates on Port Talbot rather than the wider County Borough of Neath Port Talbot that has existed since 1996.

[7] Exceptions are Swansea's Paul Ferris, *Richard Burton*, New English Library edition, 1984, and Gethin Matthews, *Richard Burton: Seren Cymru*, Gwasg Gomer, 2002.

[8] See Rees, *Real Port Talbot*, pp. 66, 99.

[9] First opened in 1839, new docks were completed in 1898. In 1885 the Rhondda and Swansea Bay Railway Company linked Aberafan with Cymmer. The Port Talbot Railway and Docks Company formed in 1894 covered thirty-five miles inland.

[10] The Borough of Port Talbot was created in 1921. After local reorganisation in 1974 it was briefly called the Borough of Afan. [11] Peter Stead, *Acting Wales: Stars of Stage and Screen*, University of Wales Press, 2002, p. 170.

[12] Glan Afan School Centenary 1896–1996, *Avonian*, p. 53, in E/PT Sec 6, WGA.

[13] Michael Sheen on *The Film Programme*, BBC Radio 4, 12 April 2012.

[14] There have been many biographies of Richard Burton, of varying quality and length. Tom Rubython, *And God Created Burton*, Myrtle Press, 2011, runs to more than 800 pages.

[15] See Peter Stead, *Richard Burton: So Much, So Little*, Seren, 1991, and Idem, *Acting Wales*, pp. 45-57.

[16] Chris Williams (ed.), *The Richard Burton Diaries*, Yale University Press, 2012. Williams does, however, discuss this first diary in his stimulating article 'Hwyl and Hiraeth: Richard Burton and Wales', *Transactions of the Honourable Society of Cymmrodorion*, 19, 2013, pp. 175–89. A forthcoming film provisionally called *Mr Burton* (produced by Josh Hyams and written by Tom Bullough) will be a drama about Richard and Philip Burton. HTV's *The Man Who Gave His Name Away* (1992) was about the latter.

[17] Quoted in the *New York Times* 18 December 2013.

[18] Stead, *Acting Wales*, p. 187.

[19] On becoming a Freeman of the Borough in 2008.

[20] www.theguardian.com/stage/2011/apr/24/the-passion-port-talbot-review

[21] *Observer* 1 May 2011.

[22] Called the Somersetshire House, it became the Somerset Arms.

[23] See www.pegentwistle.co.uk; Rees, *Real Port Talbot*, p. 44; James Zeruk, *Peg Entwistle and the Hollywood Sign Suicide*, McFarland, 2013; Hope Anderson, *Peg Entwistle and the Hollywood Sign*, BookBaby ebook, 2013.

[24] Crazyhorse Productions, Granville Theatre, Ramsgate, Kent, October 2014.

[25] Obituary in the *Wayfarer,* July 1943.

[26] Ibid, Lent, 1933.

[27] Philip Burton, *Early Doors: My Life and the Theatre*, The Dial Press, 1969, p. 190.

[28] http://www.theatricalia.com/play/2/hamlet/production/7ce, Old Vic, London 1936–7, University of Bristol.

[29] Alan Strachan, *Secret Dreams: A Biography of Michael Redgrave*, Weidenfeld & Nicolson, 2004, p. 129.

[30] *The Times* 4 June 1937.

[31] A photograph in *The Annotated Shakespeare*, A. L. Rowse ed., volume 111, Orbis, 1978, p. 265, shows Hamlet and Laertes with swords drawn. The caption identifies them as Olivier and Owen Jones in 1936. However, the same photograph is reproduced in Logan Gorlay, (ed.), *Olivier*, Weidenfeld & Nicolson, 1973, plate section, where we are told that it shows Olivier 'as Hamlet with Michael Redgrave as Laertes, 1937'. Other photographs of both Owen Jones and Michael Redgrave give the impression that it was Redgrave rather than the Welshman but Burton saw the Shakespeare volume and accepted it as Owen Jones (Philip Burton, *Richard & Philip: The Burtons*, Peter Owen, 199, p. 17).

[32] www.bryn-porttalbot.btck.co.uk/BrynPastandPresent/Owen JonesActor

[33] Gareth Elwyn-Jones and Gordon Wynne Roderick, *A History of Education in Wales*, University of Wales Press, 2003, p. 131. Pupils in Wales were also much more likely to be receiving their education free of charge.

[34] Leslie Evans, *The Story of Taibach and District*, published privately, 1963, p. 81.

[35] Gilbertson & Co. of Pontardawe established the Port Talbot Iron and Steel Company in 1901–2 on land leased by Emily Talbot. It failed within a year but was succeeded by the Port Talbot Steel Company in 1906 owned by Baldwins Ltd. and the Gloucester Railway Carriage & Wagon Co. In 1916 the wartime government subsidised the building of the Margam Steelworks, thus ensuring a source of pig iron for Baldwin's.

[36] I shall refer to the young Richard Burton as Richard/Richard Jenkins because this was his correct name at the time and to avoid confusion with Philip Burton.

[37] For the significance of being a scholarship pupil see Mavis Nicolson's account. She came from nearby Briton Ferry and won a place at Neath Grammar School. Mavis Nicolson, *Martha Jane and Me. A Girlhood in Wales*, Seren, 2008 edition.

[38] He was Tom Howell. Quoted in Ferris, *Richard Burton*, p. 13.

[39] 'The Magic of Meredith Jones', *Sunday Times* 17 June 1956.

[40] Ibid.

[41] Stead, *So Much, So Little*, p. 98.

[42] Rhys Davies Papers, NLW MS. R2/3, 7 January 1970, NLW. His mother was forty-five when his father died and had to live on 30/- a week. She was Somerset-born but grew up in Wales. Her second husband (Burton's father) was from a middle-class Staffordshire family. He became a collier on moving to Wales. D. A. Callard, 'The Other Philip Burton', *Planet*, 122, 1977, pp. 90–97.

[43] P. H. Burton to Hubert Davies, 25 February 1992, private correspondence.

[44] *Wayfarer*, Lent, 1933.

[45] Burton, *Early Doors*, p. 44.

[46] Quoted in John Davies, 'John Davies and the WEA in the Inter-War Years' in Joe England (ed.), *Changing Lives: Workers' Education in Wales 1907-2007*, Llafur, 2007, p. 42.

[47] The WEA continued to be a significant provider of classes in Port Talbot. In the mid-1950s it was at the centre of a pilot scheme (run in just three areas in Britain) to develop its work with trade unions. See Joe England, 'Working with the Unions 1945–1975' in Idem, *Changing Lives*, pp. 117–37.

[48] J. Ivor Hanson, *Profile of a Welsh Town*, published privately, 1968, p. 142.

[49] Evans, *The Story of Taibach*, p.188.

[50] Allan Cook, unpublished talk on 'The English Theatre in Wales'; National Fairground Archive, University of Sheffield www.nfa.dept.shef.ac.uk; Ian Parsons, *Swansea's Grand*, Bryngold Books, 2010, p.137. Ted Ebley was presented with a gold watch for his services to entertainment in the borough.

[51] Originally called the Aberavon and Port Talbot District YMCA (Young Men's Christian Association).

[52] See Ibid, *Profile of a Welsh Town*, p.108; *PTG* 27 July 1966.

[53] The YMCA started in Clarence Street and moved to Station Road in 1919.

[54] *PTG* 20 March 1942.

[55] Ibid.

[56] A separate YWCA existed in the centre of town.

[57] First produced there in October 1938.

[58] *PTG* 8, 15 May 1942.

[59] *Wayfarer*, 1990.

[60] Conversation between Rosalie Mahoney and Enfys McMurry, 27 September 2014.

[61] *Wayfarer*, Michaelmas Term 1938, p. 21.

[62] See, for example, Michael Munn, *Richard Burton: Prince of Players*, JR Books, 2008, Chapter 3, and Roger Lewis's article: www.telegraph.co.uk/culture/11012980/why-Richard-Burton-should-be-reburied-in-wales.html.

[63] *Daily Mirror* 24 October 1977 in RWB/1/9/1, RBP.

[64] *Guardian* 23 September 1972. One biography suggests that he was brought up on lava [sic] bread and that his family spoke an ancient Celtic Welsh called Cymric. Another claims that he took on a new name to escape from the Rhondda. Ruth Waterbury, *Richard Burton: His Intimate Story*, Mayflower-Dell, 1965; Penny Junor, *Burton: The Man Behind the Myth*, Sidgwick & Jackson, 1985.

[65] Quoted in Williams (ed.), *The Richard Burton Diaries*, p. 30. The diary began on 10 December 1939 just after the death of a sister-in-law.

[66] Aberavon Rugby Football Club Centenary booklet 1876–1976, p. 88. Richard Burton contributed an article to this booklet (pp. 68–72). It ended with him pledging lifelong allegiance to his town and its rugby team.

[67] According to his *Guardian* article 23 September 1972.

[68] A literal translation is 'the shithouse' but, as Sally Roberts Jones points out, 'the fleapit' is a more appropriate English term for this popular but basic cinema. Sally Roberts Jones, 'Beyond the Picturedrome: Port Talbot and the cinema', *New Welsh Review*, ix/1/33, Summer 1996, p. 56.

[69] David Berry, *Wales and Cinema*, University of Wales Press, 1971, p.172.

[70] *PTG* 22 March 1940.

[71] Ibid 17 November 1941.

[72] Established in 1933 as a breakaway from Gibeon Chapel (which Richard and the James family had attended until then), it met first in the minister's home in Park View, then in Taibach Library, securing its own premises in 1939.

[73] Williams (ed.), *The Richard Burton Diaries*, p. 63.

[74] In an interview with Kenneth Tynan. See Williams, 'Hwyl and Hiraeth', 19, 2013, p. 175.

[75] *The Bridge* 3, July 1943, pp. 7–8 in Leslie Evans Papers, D/D LE 466, WGA.

[76] See the conversation reported between brothers Verdun and Graham in Matthews, *Richard Burton*, p. 28.

[77] For the town's array of libraries see John V. Hughes, 'The History of Libraries in the Port Talbot District, *Port Talbot Historian*, 1V/2, 2000, pp. 108–37.

[78] Graham Jenkins, *Richard Burton, My Brother*, Michael Joseph, 1988, pp. 29–30.

[79] See Peter Stead's stimulating essay 'Bloody Welshman' in Idem, *Richard Burton*, pp. 91–123.

[80] Chris Williams, 'Richard Burton, aspirant scholar', unpublished paper, Swansea University 2010; Idem, 'What Piece of Work Was Richard Burton?' in H. V. Bowen (ed.), *A New History of Wales: Myths and Realities in Welsh History*, Gomer, 2011, pp. 174–9.

[81] Williams (ed.), *The Richard Burton Diaries*, p. 41.

[82] www.humphreylyttleton.com/a-romantic-socialist/port-talbot/

[83] www.francisfrith.com/pontrhydyfen/growing-up-in-morgans-terrace_memory-236421 by Rhys John Emmanuel, Ivor's brother who survived and later emigrated to New Zealand. Ivor was raised by his Aunt Flossie.

[84] This account is partly based on the *Wayfarer* volume covering 1916–62.

[85] P. H. Burton writing in *Wayfarer*, Michaelmas 1947.

[86] Reminiscences of Betty Rees, who acted in the play, quoted in David Roberts (ed.) *A Century of Dyffryn School: Fulfilment through Education*, Bryngold Books, 2012, p. 67.

[87] Philip Burton, *Richard & Philip*, p. 15.

[88] *Wayfarer*, Summer 1938, p. 15.

[89] *The Bridge* 3, July 1943, pp. 3–4; *PTG* 12 September 1941.

[90] *PTG* 23 October 1942.

[91] Evans, *The Story of Taibach and District*, p. 12; Idem 'Some Reminiscences of Richard Burton' in DD/LE 195/5, WGA.

[92] Ibid.

[93] First performed in 2004.

[94] Burton, 'The Magic of Meredith Jones'.

[95] David Jenkins, *Richard Burton: A Brother Remembered*, Arrow Books, 1994, p. 27.

[96] *GG* 5 May 1939. Evan Morgan was in this.

[97] Quoted in John Cottrell and Fergus Cashin, *Richard Burton: An Intimate Biography*, Arthur Barker, 1971, p. 43. See Chapter 2 below.

[98] The Taibach and Port Talbot Co-operative Society had been founded by local steelworkers and their families in 1902 and remained independent until 1996 when it became part of the Co-operative Retail Society.

[99] Although described in official documents as a coal hewer, he was known as Dic Bach y Saer – Little Dick the (colliery) carpenter. According to brother David he later worked as a plate-layer for the Great Western Railway. Jenkins, *Richard Burton*, p. 3.

[100] It was one of the Centre's favourite plays, performed on a number of occasions in the Port Talbot area.

[101] Evans, 'Some reminiscences'.

[102] In autumn 1940 they acted in *Macbeth* in Neath. Pupils from Neath Intermediate School and the Technical School were treated to a special matinée. *PTG* 1 November 1940.

[103] Quoted in Jonathan Croall, *Sybil Thorndike: A Star of Life*, Haus Publishing, 2008, p. 318.

[104] *Wayfarer*, Michaelmas, 1941, p. 4.

[105] The four houses were named after Welsh Lords of Glamorgan. Leisan became a Lord at the age of eighty in 1208, dying five years later. He gave land to Margam Abbey.

[106] *Wayfarer*, December 1942, p. 31.

[107] Burton's play about the 'San Demetrio' oil tanker set on fire but brought home by its crew was based on the account told to him by Charles Pollard of Port Talbot, the tanker's chief engineer.

[108] *Wayfarer*, July 1943, p. 32.

[109] Reproduced in Matthews, *Richard Burton*, opposite p. 100.

[110] *Wayfarer*, December 1942, p. 20.

[111] Ferris, *Richard Burton*, p. 28.

[112] P. H. Burton, *White Collar*, printed by W. H. Smith, 1938, p. 49.

[113] Williams (ed.), *The Richard Burton Diaries*, p. 511, 6 November 1971.

[114] Burton, *Open Doors*, p. 41.

[115] See Matthews, *Richard Burton*, p. 34.

[116] Burton, *Richard and Philip*, p. 16.

[117] Http://www.oxforddnb.com/view/article/59312, accessed 8 March 2015.

[118] He was a member of Hampstead Labour Party. *Empire News and Sunday Chronicle* 16 November 1958 in Leslie Evans Papers, WGA.

[119] Ibid.

[120] Letter to Brinley Jenkins, WA/10/102, 31 October 1949 – Jenkins, Brinley-Radio Artists pre-1970, BBC Written Archives Centre, Caversham Park, Reading.

[121] Stead, *So Much, So Little*, p. 120.

[122] Burton, *Early Doors*, p. 84.

[123] Melvyn Bragg's authorised and acclaimed *Rich: The Life of Richard Burton*, Hodder & Stoughton, 1988, p. 33 shows that not only was

Philip Burton's memoir originally entitled *The Two Burtons* but also that the manuscript was written in the mid-80s. Not long after Bragg visited Burton the latter decided against publishing it – perhaps because not much time had elapsed since Richard's death – but, persuaded by David Callard, he later changed his mind.

[124] *GG* 26 August, 9 September 1938.

[125] www.bbc.co.uk/news/uk-wales-17780171.

[126] *Wayfarer*, December 1942, p. 7.

[127] See Stead, *Richard Burton*, pp. 108–116 on Burton's Anglo-Welsh voice. The youth had discovered (and been mightily impressed by) Dylan Thomas' poetry before Philip Burton and Emlyn Williams.

[128] Alec Nisbett: www.bbc.co.uk/news/entertainment-arts 28964735.

[129] Peter Stead, *Film and the Working Class: The Feature Film in British and American Society*, Routledge, 1991 edition, p. 189.

[130] Burton, *Richard & Philip*, p. 21.

[131] Idem, *Early Doors*, p. 82.

[132] P. H. Burton, *Granton Street*, printed by W. H. Smith, 1934.

[133] Ibid, p. 16.

[134] Ibid, p. 56.

[135] Entry for Richard Burton in online Dictionary of Welsh Biography: http://yba.llgc.org.uk/en/s8-BURT-RIC-1925.html.

[136] See Tony Palmer's *In From The Cold? A Portrait of Richard Burton*, Isolde Films, 2009.

[137] Draft typescript 'Aberavon and Rugby' in RWB/1/2/1/4, RBP. [138] It is unsigned but it seems that this typescript in the RBP was the account that Philip Burton was told about but never read. It is shorter than the ten pages referred to by Burton (Burton, *Richard & Philip*, p. 123) but the use of the familiar Phil and references to Aaron (Aaron Frosch – Richard Burton's lawyer) and to Jim Benton (his personal assistant) and other internal evidence suggest that this critique was by Richard. Burton made no alterations in response to it. This increases the likelihood that it was the same document as the one that he was not permitted to read. RWB/1/12/1, RBP.

[139] Burton, *Richard & Philip*, pp. 22, 29.

[140] *PTG* 22 October 1943.

[141] Recording of the service of Thanksgiving for Richard Burton CBE, 30 August 1984, personal collection.

[142] Compare this with Philip Burton's stage directions for *Granton Street* stressing that the working-class characters in his play should not talk like 'Stage Welshmen' but speak 'plain English'. Burton, *Granton Street*, p. 2.

[143] *Wayfarer*, bound edition, volume IV.

[144] He changed his name to Burton by deed poll.

[145] *Wayfarer*, July 1945.

[146] Rhys Davies claimed never to have visited Port Talbot. See Meic Stephens, *Rhys Davies: A Writer's Life*, Parthian, 2013, p. 246. The two men later enjoyed an epistolary transatlantic friendship.

[147] In a letter to Rhys Davies, Rhys Davies Papers, MS. R2/3, 30 October 1957, NLW. Burton supported Sybil when the marriage broke up but remained close to Richard in later years. At Richard's request he rescued *Camelot* after Moss Hart had a heart attack. He spent three hectic weeks preparing the show for Boston and New York, savouring its subsequent success. Ibid, 13 December 1960.

[148] Letter to David Callard, NLW MS 23545D, 31 January 1991, NLW.

[149] As he recalled in a talk in Port Talbot years later. *PTG* 18 October 1979.

[150] Patrick Hannan, *The Welsh Illusion*, Seren, 2004 edition, p. 51.

[151] http://www.plazaporttalbot.co.uk.

[152] Baldwins and Guest Keen and Nettlefold merged in 1930.

[153] For further information about the Works see Stephen Parry, 'History of the Steel Industry in the Port Talbot Area 1900–1988', Ph.D., Leeds University, 2011.

[154] *GG* 7 January 1955. See too the figure of Uncle Bryn in Owen Sheers, *The Gospel Of Us*, NTW, 2011.

[155] See Rees, *Real Port Talbot*, p. 52.

[156] This letter and the following material about Jenkins and Hopkins is, unless otherwise noted, from the private archive of Fred Steadman-Jones. See too Quentin Falk, *Anthony Hopkins: The Authorised Biography*, Virgin, 2000 edition, pp. 14–15; Michael Feeney Callan, *Anthony Hopkins: In Darkness and Light*, Pan, 1994 edition, pp. 45–8; Scrapbook, D/D LE 144, Leslie Evans Papers, WGA.

[157] *GG* 25 February 1955.

[158] One of his first roles appears to have been as the butler in the comedy-thriller *Hawk Island* for the Port Talbot Repertory Players.

[159] Madame Miriam Joseph was another Port Talbot elocutionist. Nesta Morgan of Penycae taught elocution to the Texan film actor Zachary Scott when he spent a summer as a student at Bath's Theatre Royal. In the 1950s she coached several Port Talbot actors who went on to drama school in London. *GG* 6 May 1955.

[160] Ibid 19, 26 August 1938.

[161] On 9 December 1938 the *Gazette* reported that Jenkins had resigned from the Little Theatre and been replaced by Glyn Pugh, who would put on Jack Jones' *Land of My Fathers*. It was not, however, until 1955 with *Children to Bless You* followed by *Antigone* the following year that the theatre began annual productions.

[162] In the 1950 Reading Festival the fourteen-year-old was deemed 'the festival's most promising competitor' and awarded a scholarship for tuition in speech and drama at the Guildhall School of Music in London. She attended whilst still a schoolgirl.

[163] In Velindre where he had been born. Velindre (Felindre, like Trefelin) means Mill Town.

[164] He was also invited by other societies in the 1950s and 60s to put on plays. They included the British Railways Amateur Dramatics Society and Porthcawl and Port Talbot Little Theatres. Clarice died in 1956 but Jenkins lived for a further seventeen years. Their daughter married Fred Steadman-Jones, who acted in and produced for the YMCA Players. As a drama lecturer in Liverpool, he and a colleague were the first to stage the work (several one-act plays) of their student Willy Russell. In 1989–90 Cyril and Clarice's only grandchild, Richard Steadman-Jones, wrote and directed (as an Oxford undergraduate) two award-winning plays for the Edinburgh Festival Fringe, garnering fulsome praise from, inter alia, Michael Billington.

[165] As he explained when given the Freedom of the Borough in 1994.

[166] John Hampden (ed.), *Eight Modern Plays*, Nelson, 1952 edition, pp. 224–5.

[167] *GG* 14 October 1955.

[168] A typed (rather than the usual printed) programme exists for a second, undated production of the play in aid of Hungarian Relief Fund. There was one cast change but Anthony Hopkins remained. Since the Hungarian Rising did not take place until late in 1956 it suggests that this version was performed at Christmas 1956. Indeed, *Bonaventure* is announced in the programme as the next production and that was staged in February 1967. Hopkins was already a student but *Emmanuel* was staged during the vacation.

[169] *PTG* 23 December 1955.

[170] *GG* 7 October 1955.

[171] Prince Frank Littler CBE (1901–73), theatre proprietor, impresario and television executive, came from an English family of theatre managers. He chaired three major theatre groups. In 1935 he purchased Cardiff's New Theatre and the Prince of Wales. He and brother Emile were especially associated with pantomimes and musicals and their charitable work. www.its-behind-you.com/Implittlers.html.

[172] Quoted in Callan, *Anthony Hopkins*, p. 52.

[173] Quoted in Falk, *Anthony Hopkins*, p. 19.

[174] Hanson, *Profile of a Welsh Town*, p. 110.

[175] He and his brother Tom (general secretary of the Transport and Salaried Staff Association) had attended the County School. Hanson, *Profile of a Welsh Town*, p. 110; Idem, *Outline of a Welsh Town*, Daffodil Publications, 1971, p. 163 and Clive Jenkins, *All Against the Collar: Struggles of a White Collar Union Leader*, Methuen, 1990.

[176] *GG* 27 May 1955.

[177] *Wayfarer* volume for1916–62.

[178] *GG* 20 January 1956.

[179] Called Gwent since 1974.

[180] It is now spelt as Glan Afan but used to be Glanafan.

[181] In 2014, just before the World Cup, Michael Sheen captained a charity Rest of the World team at Old Trafford against England (captained by the singer Robbie Williams) for Soccer Aid.

[182] Jackie McGlone, 22 May 1993: ww.heraldscotland.com/sport/spl/aberdeen/a-wizard-coming-in-from-the-wings-1.758465

[183] Notably John Beale Director of Education and his deputy Clayton Heycock.

[184] *PTG* 22 October 1943.

[185] The Welsh-medium youth movement (founded in 1922), it holds its own National Eisteddfod.

[186] *GG* 27 April 1956.

[187] Recounted to Kevin Matherick, former head of drama at Sandfields.

[188] Sandfields County Secondary School had previously put on school plays.

[189] Not to be confused with the Cardiff-born actor Matthew Rhys.

[190] Derek Cobley directed WGYTC for eight years. Since 2000 an Artistic Directorate has been running it with eleven experienced Youth Theatre tutors.

[191] Radio 3, *Private Passions*, 26 January 2014.

[192] According to the family trees compiled by John Sheen; BBC Wales *Coming Home*, 24 November 2010.

[193] John Sheen, 'Who Was Mary Ann North?' unpublished paper.

[194] See Chapter 4 for more about this society. 1927 saw an internal schism so for twenty years there were two societies, the old one and the Afan and District.

[195] See the *Sunday Times Magazine* 1 March 2015.

[196] She trained at the Guildford School of Acting after working with the National Youth Theatre of Wales and Gwent Young People's Theatre. She has had lead roles on the London stage, was Jennifer Gabriel in the world première of *The Witches of Eastwick* and toured the US in the title role of Mary Poppins.

[197] This earned an Ian Charleson nomination. Stead in *Acting Wales*, p. 170, sees his Henry V as identifying Sheen as 'one of the most powerful actors of the era'. Richard Burton had famously played Henry V at Stratford in 1951. After he died, the Adrian Noble RSC production starring Kenneth Branagh dedicated a performance to the actor's memory, attended by the Jenkins family.

[198] John James Price, 'Through Grace——By Faith', unpublished typescript. The school leaving age was fourteen but he was given formal permission to leave at thirteen since he could prove real

family need. The school term ended before his thirteenth birthday, hence starting work aged twelve.

199 *Old Port Talbot and District in Photographs*, vol. 2, 1982, Port Talbot Historical Society, Plate 60 shows crowds gathered outside Bethany Chapel for the start of a walking race from Port Talbot to Pyle in 1903.

200 When asked for a publication whether being a Welshman had resulted in being typecast – hardly a problem for Sheen – he responded by explaining that the only time he has portrayed Welsh characters he has elected to do this as, for example, making Norman a Welshman in *The Dresser* (in the Drum Theatre, Plymouth in a production he directed himself in 1995). Joanna Davies, *Taff Pac*, Y Lolfa, 2000, p. 27.

201 Parry, 'History of the Steel Industry', Chapter 8.

202 An additional problem was Port Talbot's late adoption of the economical BOS system that used basic oxygen top-blown converters. When this was finally used in 1969, 2,000 men lost their jobs. Ibid, p. 146.

203 Ibid, Chapter 8; Steven Stokes, 'Port Talbot Steelworks: An Industry's Influence on a Town', *Cambria* 13/1, 2011–2, p. 9.

204 Parry, 'History of the Steel Industry', p. 220. See Chapters 10 and 11 for this period.

205 C. C. Harris, *Redundancy and Recession in South Wales*, Basil Blackwell, 1987, p. 86.

206 This competitive award (with drama schools each nominating two candidates) was established in 1997 by the Society of London Theatre to commemorate Olivier's eightieth birthday. In 1998 Sheen was nominated for the Laurence Olivier Award for Best Supporting Performance (for *Amadeus* at London's Old Vic). He was also nominated on three occasions for the Laurence Olivier Award for Best Actor: in 1999 *(Look Back in Anger* at the National Theatre, London), in 2003 *(Caligula)* and in 2006 *(Frost/Nixon)*, both at the Donmar Warehouse.

207 *Guardian* 7 August 1991.

208 *Observer* 8 March 1992.

209 Ibid 6 March 1994.

210 Michael Winterbottom's *The Trip* (BBC 2, 2010) was also a feature film.

[211] Quoted in Michael Odell's interview in *The Times* 13 November 2014.

[212] Deleted scenes from the series include a section about Sheen, with Rob Brydon declaring that 'he's in the line of Burton and Hopkins'.

[213] Sustrans is a UK charity promoting healthy, sustainable forms of transport. See Rees, *Real Port Talbot*, p. 86.

[214] Another Port Talbot comedian (ex-Glan Afan) is the Jewish-Welsh Bennett Arron, a winner of the TAPS Comedy Writer of the Year Award. He studied at the Academy of Live and Recording Arts in London and taught drama for two years. *SWEP* 23 January 2001.

[215] Eddie Izzard also briefly attended Porthcawl Comprehensive.

[216] In 1997 he won a Tony on Broadway for his Torvald in Ibsen's *A Doll's House*.

[217] Rob Brydon, *Small Man in a Book*, Michael Joseph, 2011, p. 113.

[218] Born in 1906 in Aberafan, the son of a Gilbert and Sullivan comic actor, Morris was a talented whistler and mimic by the age of ten. A tinplate worker then travelling salesman, he performed in clubs and concert parties. He turned professional, was the resident comedian on Welsh Rarebit, and starred in British Variety Shows. Brian Jones, *Port Talbot: A Gallery of Past Personalities* 3, privately printed, 1992, pp. 35–41.

[219] Ibid, p. 120.

[220] www.walesonline.co.uk/lifestyle/showbiz/rob-brydon-impressions-sir-anthony-hopkins-6952002.

[221] Quoted in Falk, *Anthony Hopkins*, p. 60.

[222] Ibid, p. 56.

[223] Callan, *Anthony Hopkins*, p. 63.

[224] See too Victor Spinetti's comments on his poetry recitations. Victor Spinetti, *Up Front*, Robson Books, 2000, pp. 151, 181.

[225] She would have acted in his production of the play for Theatr Clwyd in Mold, north Wales but was unwell during rehearsals, so had to be replaced.

[226] In 1992 it was reprised as 'An Evening with Dylan Thomas' to raise funds for the Prince's Trust.

[227] 'The Richard Burton Legacy', BBC Radio 2, 12 August 2010.

228 Ibid.

229 Ibid.

230 *Independent* 16 July 1999.

231 'The Richard Burton Legacy'.

232 Stead, *Acting Wales*, p. 171.

233 *Private Passions*, Radio 3, 26 January 2014.

234 Burton's voice was used again in 1963 and posthumously in 2003. In 1972 Andrew Sinclair's film adaptation with Burton (and Elizabeth Taylor) was shot in Fishguard, Pembrokeshire. Guy Masterson has produced and performed his own solo version of the play on numerous occasions.

235 BBC Wales, 5 May 2014.

236 *Wales Arts Review* 3/9, 2014.

237 'The Richard Burton Legacy'.

238 BBC Radio Wales, 26 October 2014; BBC Radio 4, *Front Row,* 22 October 2014.

239 Made by Presentable Productions/BBC Wales.

240 'An Audience with Michael Sheen', BAFTA Cymru in London 17 March 2015.

241 *South Wales Echo and Express,* 16 June 1955.

242 'Babylon Wales. Notes from the margins of Welsh popular culture' by Anthony Brockway, 23 November 2008. www.babylonwales.blogspot.co.uk/2008/11/ronald-lewis.html.

243 Information about Rees comes from his descendants and from Peter Whitebrook, author of *John Osborne: Anger is not About...* , Oberon, 2015.

244 Letter from Philip Burton WA/10/102 Jenkins, Brinley-Radio Artists pre-1970, 31 October 1949, BBC Written Archives, Caversham.

245 *PTG* 22 October 1943.

246 *Argus* 11 June 2012.

247 Siân Phillips noted in her autobiography that many character actors had 'day' jobs: 'An awful lot of Welsh solicitors had equity cards.' Siân Phillips, *Private Faces: The Autobiography*, Hodder Sceptre edition, 1999, p. 268.

248 *PTG* 22 October 1943.

[249] Ibid 6 June 1941.

[250] They include the Afan Arts Centre and the Afan Lido. Charles B. Tapp, Ina Jones and J. Edward John were amongst its most dedicated and talented actor-producers.

[251] This drama group of the Dyffryn Afan and Margam Cymrodorion Society put on plays in Aberafan's New Hall and the YMCA. They also entered dramas such as the comedy John a Jâms (John and James) at the National Eisteddfod.

[252] *PTG* 11 April 1941, 20 March 24 April, 20 June 1942; *GG* 23 September 1955. Philip Burton had little time for him though conceded that he had 'some acting ability' in 'unpleasant neurotic parts'. It seems that Blackwell claimed to have worked under Burton, which the latter denied. Philip Burton, letter to Rhys Davies in Rhys Davies Papers, R2/3, 11 October 1947, NLW.

[253] Singing Welsh verses in counterpoint to a traditional harp melody.

[254] Phillips, *Private Faces*, p. 47.

[255] Rhydfelen near Pontypridd, opened in 1962.

[256] A former nurse who had been in the West Glamorgan Youth Choir and trained at the Guildhall School of Music and Drama, her father was a local actor and producer. Her mother had been in Ivor Novello's theatre company.

[257] Mavis Richards (née Smollett) the choreographer was related to Blythe. Another local singer Evelyn Stevenson took part in Ivor Novello shows in London.

[258] Dillwyn's mother was Elfed James' sister. James was also connected to the Dummer family by marriage. She married Edwin Dummer who was the brother of Jae Alexander's grandfather and also brother of Catherine (Phyllis) Dolan's mother.

[259] This award-winning film was re-released in 2004 as *Small Miracles*.

[260] www.theatre-wales.co.uk/plays/review_archive.asp?playname =A%20kiss%20on%20the%20Bottom&company=Sherman%20Theatre%20Company. See too *SWEP* 19 September 2013, 3 May 2014.

[261] In the same year group was Andrew Morgan who now runs the successful Andy Morgan Casting Agency.

[262] See Gerard Gilbert's interview with Salford's Christopher Eccleston in *i* 18 April 2015.

[263] *SWEP* 5 October 2013.

[264] *Neil Diamond* – One Night Only, ITV 1, 13 November 2014.

[265] Martin Johnes, *Wales since 1939*, Manchester University Press, 2012, p. 79.

[266] 'Who Cares about Wales? I Care', *Look*, 24 June 1969.

[267] Williams, 'Hwyl and Hiraeth', p. 176.

[268] Ibid, p. 179.

[269] Years of keen longing.

[270] For this section see Menna Gallie, 'The Two Valleys' L1/2 in the Menna Gallie Archive at NLW.

[271] Graham Jenkins spent some years working for the BBC in London, thanks partly to his brother's assistance.

[272] In RWB /1/2/1/9, RBP.

[273] Oseagram, 16 February 1972, personal collection.

[274] Five years later Graham Jenkins became the manager of the Afan Lido.

[275] For Pontrhydyfen as the point of reference in the diaries from the 1960s see, for example, 13 November 1968 (with Taylor the 'Princess of Pontrhydyfen') and 8 July 1970, Williams (ed.), *The Richard Burton Diaries*, pp. 224, 396.

[276] *GG* 7 January 1955.

[277] Ibid 25 February 1955.

[278] Ibid 20 January 1956.

[279] See the novel by Jess Walter, *Beautiful Ruins*, Penguin, 2012, also Roger Lewis, *Erotic Vagrancy*, forthcoming, 2015.

[280] Sam Kashner and Nancy Schoenborger, *Furious Love: Elizabeth Taylor and Richard Burton*, JR Books, 2010.

[281] RWB/1/2/1/9, RBP.

[282] Ibid, RWB/1/3/1. See Appendix.

[283] *Daily Telegraph* 26 July 2007.

[284] *Stage* 23 July 2007. See too *Independent* 24 July 2007; *Guardian* 17 August 2007.

[285] Also from a Welsh mining background and helped by a teacher (Glynne Morse) but not, as is claimed in Geoffrey Macnab, 'Valley Boys', *Sight and Sound* 4/3, 1994, pp. 20-3, from the same area. Baker was from the Rhondda and his father was a disabled miner.

See *Observer* 11 July 1976 for Burton's obituary of him. He was godfather to Baker's daughter.

[286] See Robert Shail, *Stanley Baker: A Life in Film*, University of Wales Press, 2008, Chapter 4.

[287] *GG* 21 October 1955.

[288] Hanson, *Profile of a Welsh Town*, p. 146.

[289] Richard Burton to Dennis Burgess, MS. 23970D, NLW.

[290] Ibid, 9 October 1967.

[291] Ibid, 6 March 1972.

[292] Ibid, Telegram, 4 March 1972.

[293] Ibid, Letter, 6 March 1972.

[294] Ibid.

[295] Ibid. Card, nd.

[296] Ibid. Letter, 28 April 1972.

[297] Ibid, 6 March 1972.

[298] Ibid, Telegram, 12 October 1972. See too Telegram, 3 November 1972.

[299] So did Brook Williams. The son of Emlyn Williams who had given Burton his first break, Williams had cameo roles in a number of Burton's films and was like an honorary member of the family. The film's release was delayed for two years.

[300] Nevertheless he was typecast anyway. An actor working with him at the Liverpool Playhouse commented that 'a lot of people could not cope with his Welshness'. Quoted in Falk, *Anthony Hopkins*, p. 29.

[301] In the event RADA put Rhys up for the Lady Rothermere Award and he won it. He returned Hopkins' money but it was given to another student. Information kindly received from Matthew Rhys and RADA.

[302] An exhibition about Burton's early life (thanks to a permanent loan from Burton's niece Rhianon Trowell) is also on display.

[303] For an account of how this came about following a Masterclass at the theatre, see Falk, *Anthony Hopkins*, pp. 237–46. The play lasted just under a month including three evenings at Cardiff's New Theatre.

[304] Falk, *Anthony Hopkins*, p. 219.

[305] www.bbc.co.uk/news/uk-wales-14246824. Interviewed by

Caroline Rigby, 22 July 2011. Compare this with his appearance on *The South Bank Show* on 29 March 1992.

³⁰⁶ www.bbc.co.uk/news/uk-wales-14246824.

³⁰⁷ http://www.youtube.com/watch?=KG2TOLaVAM4.

³⁰⁸ The others are Daniel Evans, Ifan Meredith, Andrew Howard and Jason Hughes. Davies, *Taff Pac*.

³⁰⁹ BBC Wales, 'Coming Home', 24 November 2010.

³¹⁰ 'Celebrating the Chartists', *Newsletter* 2, December 2013.

³¹¹ See Ibid, 3, February 2014 for details of ReNewport and plans for regeneration.

³¹² *Michael Sheen's Valleys Rebellion*, BBC Two Wales, 24 February 2015; *Western Mail* 21 February 2015.

³¹³ Interview on *The Andrew Marr Show*, BBC 1, 8 March 2015.

³¹⁴ *Western Mail* 4 January 2014.

³¹⁵ Sheen would star in *Hamlet* at the Young Vic Theatre soon after *The Passion*.

³¹⁶ He chaired from March 1975 what was initially called the Afan Community Association. Ten years later he was moved to a parish in Newport, Gwent though remained an active supporter of the play.

³₁₇ In 1987 Alan Davies co-directed with Ina Jones. From 1997 a production team of six (including Ken Tucker) was in charge.

³¹⁸ Elizabeth Robins, *Both Sides of the Curtain*, William Heinemann, 1940, p. 313.

³¹⁹ Unpublished paper by Sally Roberts Jones.

³²⁰ *Private Passions*.

³²¹ Ina Jones' words in the Foreword to the 1997 Programme.

³²² *Western Mail* 7 January 2012.

³²³ They were Matthew Aubrey, Jordan Bernarde, Di Botcher, Darren Lawrence, Jean-Paul Macleod, Rhys Matthews, Francine Morgan, Kristian Phillips, Kyle Rees, David Rees Talbot and Michael Sheen.

³²⁴ Foreword to Owen Sheers, *The Gospel Of Us*, Seren, 2012.

³²⁵ *The Big Issue,* 945, 18–24 April 2011, pp. 8–12.

³²⁶ Chris Morash and Shaun Richards, *Mapping Irish Theatre: Theories of Space and Place*, Cambridge University Press, 2013, Chapter 7, 'Theatre of the Street', p. 168.

[327] *Western Mail* 7 January 2012.

[328] Foreword to Sheers, *The Gospel Of Us*.

[329] Lucy Davies, 'How Big Is Your Town?' *National Theatre Wales*, Spring, 2012.

[330] DVD, *The Gospel Of Us*, 2012. Quoted in 'Extras'.

[331] Dylan Moore, 'Performing Wales', *Planet*, 205, 2012, p. 77.

[332] *Western Mail* 7 January 2012.

[333] The lowest estimates I have seen were for 12,000 and the highest 25,000.

[334] A term used by Donna Tartt in Idem, *The Little Friend*, Alfred A. Knopf, 2002, Chapter 4 to describe how, over time, memories in communities become automatic and irrevocable.

[335] Jasper Rees: www.bbc.co.uk/blogs/wales/posts/michael_sheen_the_Passion_reviews_round_up.

[336] Owen Sheers, 'Write of Passage' in *The Passion Memory*, Official Programme, Port Talbot Magnet, 2012, p. 26.

[337] NTW's ambitious site-specific performances have included *Mametz* in Llancayo Upper Wood near Usk, Monmouthshire in the summer of 2014. This was inspired by Owen Sheer's poem 'Mametz Wood' about the First World War battle with its high toll of Welsh casualties.

[338] *Western Mail* 7 January 2012.

[339] Davies, 'How Big Is Your Town?'

[340] *Guardian* 24 April 2011.

[341] *Independent* 1 May 2011.

[342] *Observer* 15 April 2012.

[343] Ibid 1 May 2011.

[344] McKean is also an illustrator, graphic designer, musician and comic book artist. Sheen has an interest in comic books.

[345] Dave McKean, 'The Gospel Of Us' in *The Passion Memory*, p. 30.

[346] Sheen and Mitchell did not work on the film at all (though Sheen acted in it).

[347] BBC Wales, Episode 1, *The Town Tells Its Story*, 5 June 2011; Episode 2 'It Has Begun', 12 June 2011.

[348] See www.Port-Talbot.com.

[349] www.theguardian.com/stage/2011/apr/24/the-passion-port-talbot-review.

[350] Sheers, Foreword to *The Gospel Of Us*.

[351] www.southwales-eveningpost.co.uk/Street-named-forgotten-actor-shared-mentor/story20819971-detail/story.html.

[352] RWB/1/5/3/13. News Reports, RBP.

[353] See www.visitnpt.co.uk and www.afanforestpark.co.uk. Unlike Hopkins and Sheen, Richard Burton was never given the Freedom of the Borough.

[354] See too www.richardburtonmuseum.weebly.com.

[355] Idem, 'Write of Passage' in *The Passion Memory*, p. 26

[356] For example, on *The Film Programme*, BBC Radio 4, 12 April 2012. The town has featured in a number of films. See Rees, *Real Port Talbot*, pp. 167–9. Interested in the relationship between screen and identity, Robert Taffurelli, a lecturer at Cardiff Metropolitan University and from Port Talbot, is writing a doctoral thesis provisionally entitled 'Looking for Port Talbot: An Analysis of Representation in National and Regional Cinema'.

[357] Gwyn Thomas, *A Few Selected Exits*, Hutchinson, 1968, p. 190.

[358] George Orwell, *The Road to Wigan Pier,* Victor Gollancz, 1937. [359] It cost the Port Talbot and District Amateur Operatic Society £30,350 to put on the Welsh premiere of *Sunset Boulevard* for five nights at The Princess Royal Theatre in April 2015.

[360] See, for example, 'Do actors need drama school?' *Sunday Times Supplement* 5 April 2015.

[361] There is a further WGYTC connection, with Ed Thomas along with Judy Gardner (former head of drama at BBC Wales) being instrumental in the development of this former Ford factory at Swansea Bay. Thomas and Mal Pope's company YJB Films is based there.

[362] Its claim, however, that 'There's never been a better time for actors from the valleys' was misplaced. Not one of the five actors (whose photographs it displays) comes from the valleys. They are from Porthcawl, North Cornelly (near Port Talbot) Aberystwyth, Cardiff and Port Talbot.

[363] *Cambria* 13/1, 2011–2, p. 11.

[364] See *Port Talbot Magnet* 4, Autumn 2014.

[365] There will be education in film and TV production management

for secondary school pupils. Neath Port Talbot College and Afan College in Margam will relocate in one college of 1,300 students as part of the regeneration of this area.

[366] They have put on about a dozen productions, giving work to small numbers of actors in the area and taking shows to different theatres from Swansea to London's King's Head Theatre.

INDEX

Index